ABOUT THE AUTHOR

John Langridge was educated at Marlborough College, Durham University, and the London School of Economics. He worked in Human Resources from 1986 until 2002, when he became an English teacher, having gained a CELTA (Certificate in English Language Teaching to Adults) at International House in London. He went on to teach English at two universities in France and three schools in the UK. Students from more than 70 countries attended his classes.

Much of his time was spent preparing his students for the Cambridge exams which are now B1 Preliminary and B2 First (formerly PET and FCE). Unable to find texts which contained most of the vocabulary on a particular topic, he wrote his own material so they could revise the target language they had learnt in previous weeks and months. He used what he had written in his classes for dictations, vocabulary exercises, and pronunciation practice; a sequence of activities that greatly improved their English and helped them do well in their exams. 150 of the texts, on a wide range of topics, and 2,250 clues, are now available as exercises in his book, 'All About Us!'.

Editing, design, typesetting and publishing by UK Book Publishing

www.ukbookpublishing.com

ISBN: 978-1-916572-22-5

ALL ABOUT US!

To my mother and father,
Valerie and Gordon

CONTENTS

. . . .

INTRODUCTION

'All About Us!' is a book of 150 vocabulary exercises, which can also be used by teachers and their students for dictations and pronunciation practice. Every exercise is on a separate page and a different topic. All the exercises comprise a text in English and 15 clues, many of which are definitions. The challenge for the student, or the reader, is to find the right words – which are somewhere in the text –for each of the clues!

'All About Us!' is intended for:

B1 level students (Intermediate), studying English as a foreign language (EFL), who are revising some of the target language they learnt earlier in the course, and learning new vocabulary.

B2 level students (Upper Intermediate), who need to learn some of the vocabulary and revise the rest. Finding many of the words and phrases on a particular topic in a single text, and studying them again, could be very helpful for revision.

Native English speakers at school, pupils who use English as an additional language (EAL), and speakers of other languages (ESOL). Why not read one or two of the texts and some of the clues, to see whether the exercises are at the right level for you, a member of your family, or someone else you know?

English teachers – who can use the book for dictations, vocabulary exercises, and pronunciation practice – and their students!

If you're a student at school, or you'd like to do a vocabulary exercise at home:

(i)   Read the text and try to understand or get the gist of it.
(ii)   Read the clues and try to understand them.
(iii)   Go back to the text and start looking for the right word or phrase for each clue.
(iv)   Find the correct word or phrase in the text and write it next to the clue.
(v)   Are you in a class with other students? Your teacher may put you into pairs (with another student), to talk about each of the clues and the sentence that contains the right word or phrase.

Are you reading or studying the book on your own?

Check the answers at the back of the book, correct your answers, and write down your score out of 15!

If you're reading this as an ebook, type the clues and your answers into a document, or write them on a piece of paper, or in a notebook. Writing everything down will help you learn and remember the vocabulary more easily than if you simply read the clues and try to think of the solutions.

The answers are listed in alphabetical order of the titles of the exercises, not numerical order. For example, the answers for 1. Leonardo da Vinci are under the letter L, and those for 2. Isaac Newton, are under I. All the titles that start with the definite article, 'The', are under the letter T.

If you're an English teacher, a sequence of three activities: dictations, vocabulary exercises, and pronunciation practice, as described below, could be very beneficial and productive for your students, helping them revise the vocabulary you've been teaching, and improve their spelling, comprehension, and pronunciation. The three activities shouldn't take long to prepare, but doing each one in turn, using only a single text and the 15 clues below it, will keep students focused, interested, and engaged for hours. There are 150 texts and 2,250 clues that can all be used in this way, so if you're short of time, material, or inspiration, this is the book for you!

Suggested Procedure

1. Dictation:

For the longer texts the teacher may choose to read (about) half the dictation in one class and the rest in the following class, before giving students the written version. For the shorter texts, the teacher could read the dictation in full in the first class, and provide students with the written version in the second class.

The teacher:

(i)   teaches students the words used for punctuation marks* in English, or revises them if this was done in a previous class.
(ii) reads every sentence twice, and includes punctuation marks where they appear in the text.
(iii) pauses whenever students need more time to write the words down, as well as before and after punctuation marks.

(iv) repeats any phrases or sentences the students ask to hear again.

(v)   gives or sends students a copy of the text, once it has been read out. All the possible spellings, of words that can be spelt/spelled! in more than one way, appear in the text, eg, yogurt / yoghurt / yoghourt.

(vi) asks the students to correct their own dictations.

*The English words for punctuation marks and their symbols should be visible for students on a screen, slide, or board, to help them learn or revise them. If they're in a list, the teacher can point at them or highlight them one by one, asking students to pronounce each in turn, and then repeating the words so they can hear them again, pronounced correctly.

2. Vocabulary Exercise:

The teacher:

(i)   explains that students should read the text and try to understand or get the gist of it.

(ii) tells students to find the correct word(s) in the text for the fifteen clues listed below it.

(iii) puts students into pairs once all of them, or at least the majority, have finished the exercise.

(iv) encourages them to compare answers and talk about each of the clues and the sentence that might contain the right answer.

(v)   goes through the answers, writes them on the screen, slide, or board, and talks about the sentence in the text the word or words appear in.

3. Pronunciation Practice:

Students pronounce all 15 answers as a choral drilling exercise, which means the whole class pronounces each word or phrase in turn. This is a shorter activity which should be an uplifting and enjoyable way of ending the sequence of activities.

The teacher:

(i)   points at, or highlights, each word on the screen, slide, or board, in turn.

(ii) listens as students pronounce the words.

(iii) pronounces the words to reinforce or correct the students' pronunciation.

(iv) listens to the students as they copy the teacher's pronunciation.

(v)   repeats (iii) and (iv) as many times as required

Learning, Revising and Remembering Vocabulary

Multiple encounters with a word and its meaning are known to help students learn, revise, and remember vocabulary. These encounters are the thoughts they have, and their actions, when they experience a word, its meaning, and its use in context, over and over again. A sequence of three activities in particular – dictations, vocabulary exercises, and pronunciation practice – provided my students with so many of these encounters, and so much variety in their use, they became an important and productive part of my classes. The activities, thoughts and actions, which included listening, reading, writing and speaking, were so numerous and varied, they also made learning vocabulary easier and more enjoyable. In the paragraphs below, some of the multiple encounters <u>with a single word or phrase</u> a student could experience – doing a dictation, a vocabulary exercise, and pronunciation practice, in sequence – have been highlighted in **bold** and *italics*.

If a teacher decides to use the text as a <u>dictation</u>, the student *listens* to the word or phrase being pronounced by the teacher, *spells* it, and *writes* it down. The teacher reads every sentence twice, so the student *listens* to the word again. Having read the dictation in full, the teacher shares a copy of it with the student, who reads the text, *sees* the word, and *realises* whether they've spelt it correctly. If they haven't, the student *corrects* the word.

Once the dictation has been corrected, the teacher moves on to the <u>vocabulary exercise.</u> The student goes through the text, or some of the text, *reads* the clue, *thinks* about what it means, and *considers* which word in the text might be the right solution for the clue. Once the word has been found, the student *copies* it, or *remembers* it, *checks* the spelling, *spells* it correctly and *writes* it down. The teacher may put students into pairs once they've done as much of the exercise as they can. If this happens, one student talks to another student about the clue, the word, and its meaning, *pronounces* it, *repeats* it (as they talk about it), and *listens* as the other student pronounces and repeats the word. The student then goes back to the text, *searches* for the right word, *sees* the word, reads the clue again, and *wonders* whether it's the right one. When the teacher finally goes through the answers, the student *listens* as the teacher pronounces the correct word or phrase again, and *reads* the words as the teacher writes them next to the clues.

The teacher starts the <u>pronunciation practice</u> by pointing at, or highlighting, the right word or phrase for each clue. The student *pronounces* the word and then the teacher pronounces it to reinforce or correct the student's pronunciation. The student *listens* to the correct pronunciation, *copies* the teacher, and *pronounces* the word again. When the process is repeated, which is always good practice, the student once again *listens* to the teacher's pronunciation, *copies it*, and *pronounces* the word.

Let's look at those thoughts and actions again:- listens, spells, writes, listens, sees, realises, corrects, reads, thinks, considers, copies, remembers, checks, spells, writes, pronounces, repeats, listens, searches, sees, wonders, listens, reads, pronounces, listens, copies, pronounces, listens, copies, and pronounces …. Multiple encounters, in all their forms, that help the student learn, revise, and remember vocabulary.

In the years they were due to take exams, my students worked hard every week, for months, at their grammar, and the sequence of three activities: dictations, vocabulary exercises, and pronunciation practice. Supplemented by past exam papers, these activities greatly improved their English, and in particular, helped them do well in FCE, the Cambridge exam which is now B2 First.

1-150

SUBJECTS AND TOPICS

....

VOCABULARY
EXERCISES

DISCOVERIES AND INVENTIONS

1. Leonardo da Vinci

Leonardo da Vinci is known as one of the greatest artists in history. He painted the Mona Lisa, the most famous painting in the world, which hangs on a wall of the Louvre in Paris. Millions of tourists go to see the painting every year. He wasn't just an artist, though. He was also an engineer, an architect, a scientist and an inventor. Perhaps most extraordinary of all were the machines and other objects that he first thought of or invented hundreds of years before anyone else. Among his inventions were flying machines, including a type of plane, a helicopter, and a parachute. He also designed tanks, a weapon similar to a machine gun, equipment for diving and swimming underwater, and a mobile bridge which moved on wheels. It's possible that he created the world's first robots as well, including one that moved like a human and another more like a car. He designed contact lenses, a type of calculator, and a clock that was more accurate than any other at the time. He may even have discovered what hurricanes and other types of weather look like, and how they move. He understood that air, although invisible, moved in the same way as water when there was a hurricane. No-one else was able to see this until satellites gave us pictures of the weather about 500 years later. Leonardo da Vinci, who was born in 1452 and died in 1519, was truly a genius.

Find the right word(s) in the text above for each of the clues below:

1. People who visit or travel to places for pleasure

2. One of the features on a mobile phone, used for working out numbers

3. A person who has extraordinary intelligence, skills, or abilities

4. An aircraft with large rotating blades instead of wings

5. A person who produces or designs something that hasn't existed before

6. Man-made objects in space which are used to send information and pictures back to earth

7. A person attached to this can jump out of a plane and land safely on the ground

8. Small, round, thin pieces of plastic that people put on their eyes to help them see better (2 words)

9. A weapon that can fire a large number of bullets very quickly (2 words)

10. Can't be seen

11. This is normally found over a road, a river or a railway

12. Storms with very strong, violent winds

13. Found something that no-one else had found before

14. Machines that can do complicated things automatically. Some of them have arms and legs that move like ours

15. Military vehicles which are armoured, (covered in metal for protection), and have large guns

/ 15

2. Isaac Newton

Isaac Newton was one of the greatest scientists in history. In 1665 he was at Cambridge University when it had to close because of a plague that had killed thousands of people in England. He returned to his mother's house in Lincolnshire, and lived there for two years. There's a story that he was sitting in the garden one day under an apple tree when an apple fell on his head. However, based on what was written years later by people who knew Newton, it's more likely that he saw an apple fall from the tree straight to the ground. He told them it made him question why the apple should fall downwards and not move sideways or upwards. He then began to think that objects like the apple must be pulled towards the Earth, and in particular, the centre of the Earth. As he developed his idea, he wondered whether the force extended much further than a short distance from our planet, and could even explain why the Moon goes round the Earth. In fact, he soon realised it could explain how all the objects in the universe are affected by the force, which became known as gravity.

Newton's discovery was followed by his three laws of motion, which were published in a book twenty years later. He is also famous for his work on light, what it does, and how white light is composed of all the colours of the rainbow. He invented a telescope that used mirrors to reflect light, and calculus, which is a type of maths to do with rates of change. None of these great achievements, though, are as well-known as the story about the apple and how it helped Newton discover gravity.

Find the right word(s) in the text above for each of the clues below:

1. The lenses in this piece of equipment make distant objects appear closer and larger

2. A disease that infects and kills a lot of people

3. A curve of different colours that appears in the sky when the sun shines through rain

4. The opposite of 'pushed'

5. Produced as a book or a magazine and sold to the public

6. This causes things to move upwards, downwards or sideways

7. A word for movement which nowadays is often preceded by the word 'slow'

8. We can see this at night because of light reflected from the Sun (2 words)

9. How much or how little things change, for example, over time or distance

10. We can see ourselves by looking in these

11. Suddenly knew something

12. The force that causes things to fall to the ground

13. Made or formed from several things

14. Scientific rules which explain how things happen

15. Thought about a particular question and tried to find an answer to it

/ 15

3. Michael Faraday

Michael Faraday was born in London in 1791 and was often hungry as a child because his family were poor. He left school at thirteen, worked in a bookshop and taught himself by reading books. At the age of twenty, he started attending lectures given by famous scientists, and before long he began his extraordinary career as a chemist. He discovered gases such as benzene, and found out how to turn a number of gases, including chlorine, into liquids, when no-one else thought it could be done. His work as a chemist became very important, but his contribution to physics was his greatest achievement.

Faraday was interested in magnets, which are pieces of metal that pull other metal objects towards them. He believed that magnets and electricity were related, and he became the first scientist to show that a magnet could produce electricity. Having made this discovery, he carried out experiments in which he managed to turn electrical energy into mechanical energy. In doing so, he invented and created the first electric motor. Faraday's invention has enabled us to make the machines that have become useful in so many ways in the modern world. There are cars on the roads and planes in the sky. We've got TVs, fridges and vacuum cleaners at home. Computers, mobile phones and hundreds of other machines have changed our lives.

In 1831 Faraday discovered in another experiment that he was able to reverse the process, and turn mechanical energy into electrical energy. He had created the dynamo, the very first type of generator, a machine that produces electricity. Modern generators now convert fossil fuels, nuclear power and renewable energy into the electricity we use every day. Michael Faraday discovered some of the most important laws of chemistry and physics, and his inventions of the electric motor and the generator were two of the greatest in history.

Find the right word(s) in the text above for each of the clues below:

1. Electrical machines that remove dirt and dust from carpets and floors (2 words)

2. Coal and oil formed millions of years ago from dead animals and plants (2 words)

3. A liquid, (and also a gas), which is used in swimming pools to keep the water clean

4. An adjective used for machines and engines

5. An adjective used for people who have very little money

6. A form of energy that can be replaced naturally so it won't run out, and can be used again

7. The opposite of 'push'

8. Do a series of things in the opposite order (3 words)

9. Food and drinks are kept cold in these, so they stay fresh

10. A noun used for something that's found or understood for the first time

11. An adjective that goes before 'energy, power, bomb, weapons, submarine' and 'waste'

12. This uses electricity, petrol or gas to make a machine or vehicle work

13. Scientific tests carried out to see what happens

14. A gas and also a liquid which is used to make plastic products

15. A noun used for something someone has done well or very well

/ 15

4. Howard Carter
···

Lord Carnarvon was very keen on horse racing and fast cars, but he became famous around the world because of his interest in ancient Egypt. In 1914 he was given the right to dig in the Valley of Kings near the city of Luxor to find the tombs of Egyptian pharaohs. He employed an archaeologist called Howard Carter to search the area, but very little of interest or value was found and in 1922 Carnarvon decided he would only finance the search for one more season. Finally, on the 4th of November 1922, Carter and his team discovered steps, and a door that he hoped would lead to the tomb of an Egyptian pharaoh called Tutankhamun. He contacted Carnarvon and asked him to come to Egypt as soon as possible.

On the 26th of November, Carnarvon, his daughter and others watched Carter open a tiny hole in the top-left corner of the door with a chisel. He used a candle to help him look through the door into a room. "Can you see anything ?" asked Carnavon. "Yes", replied Carter, "wonderful things!"

When they opened the door and entered the room, they found priceless gold and ebony treasures. At one end there was a sealed door, with two statues of soldiers guarding it. This door led to another room where they found the tomb of Tutankhamun. It was almost intact, and the room contained hundreds of objects, many of them covered in gold, or painted in beautiful colours. They had been placed there because it was believed the young pharaoh would need his possessions in the afterlife.

Find the right word(s) in the text above for each of the clues below:

1. Extremely valuable

2. The rulers of ancient Egypt

3. A tool with a sharp, flat end, used for cutting wood, stone or metal

4. Someone who looks for, and examines, old objects or buildings buried in the ground

5. Closed

6. Examine a particular place to find something

7. Complete and not damaged

8. Make holes in the ground (to search for something)

9. Found something that had not been found before

10. A large grave normally built of stone where an important person is buried

11. We walk up these to get to a higher level, or down them to reach a lower level

12. A wax object with a piece of string in the middle called a wick. If the wick is lit, it lights up a room

13. Protecting someone or something from danger

14. Hard, black wood from tropical trees

15. These are made of stone or metal and are usually of people or animals

/ 15

5. Alexander Fleming

Alexander Fleming was a doctor and researcher who worked in a laboratory in the basement of St Mary's Hospital in London. On the 28th of September 1928 he returned to work after a holiday with his family at their house in the country. He started sorting through some small, round dishes, sealed with lids, that he had placed in a pile before he went on holiday. The glass dishes contained a type of bacteria, tiny living things, some of which cause disease, that are visible only under a microscope. One of the dishes had been left open by mistake, and when Fleming looked at it he noticed something very strange. A blue-green mould, a type of fungus similar to a mushroom, had grown in the dish in a circle, and destroyed the bacteria around it. If it could kill bacteria in a dish, Fleming realised it might be able to kill bacteria that cause disease in humans and animals. He managed to grow the mould on its own and discovered it produced a substance that destroyed a range of different bacteria. He called the substance penicillin, but didn't think it could be produced in large enough quantities, or last long enough in the human body, to treat infection. In the 1940s, however, other scientists showed this could be done, and penicillin was one of a number of antibiotics that changed the world of medicine forever. The substance discovered by Fleming became a drug that saves millions of lives every year.

Find the right word(s) in the text above for each of the clues below:

1. Found something that had not been found before

2. Can be seen

3. A flat or shallow container

4. A type of vegetable that can be cooked and eaten

5. This means the same as 'by accident' (2 words)

6. A number of things that have been put on top of each other

7. What a person, animal or plant has when it's caused by harmful bacteria

8. The tops or covers of containers that can be removed by turning or lifting them

9. A room or building used for scientific experiments and tests

10. Penicillin is one type of these substances. They can kill bacteria and cure infection

11. A person who studies a particular subject to discover new facts or information about it

12. Give medical help to a person with an illness or an injury

13. A room or rooms in a building that are below ground level

14. Closed

15. Examining and arranging a number of things, to put them in order, or to find something (2 words)

/ 15

6. Matilda
....

Matilda, (who was born in 1102), was the daughter of King Henry I / the first of England. She left England when she was still a child, and married King Henry V / the fifth of Germany, who was also Holy Roman Emperor. In 1116 she travelled to Italy with her husband, and was crowned empress in a church in Rome. When Henry died in 1125, Matilda went to live in Normandy, which is in France, where she married Geoffrey of Anjou. Her father, Henry I/ the first, wanted her to rule England after him, but on his death in 1135, her cousin, Stephen, with the backing of the Church, became king. Matilda believed she had a better claim to the throne than her cousin, and in 1139, determined to do something about it, she returned to England. Supported by her half-brother, Robert of Gloucester, and her uncle, David I/ the first, king of Scotland, her army fought a civil war against Stephen's.

When Stephen was captured at the Battle of Lincoln in 1141, it was decided that Matilda should be crowned queen of England at Westminster, but opposition from people in London prevented the coronation from taking place. Soon afterwards Robert was also captured, but he was released when Matilda agreed to an exchange and allowed Stephen to go free as well. The war continued.

That winter she was staying at Oxford Castle when it was attacked and surrounded by Stephen's army. According to a popular story of the time, Matilda saw the snow falling heavily outside and realised enemy soldiers might not see her if she tried to escape wearing white clothes. When it was dark, dressed in white and accompanied by a number of knights, she was lowered down the castle walls. Once she reached the snow-covered ground, she crossed the frozen River Isis and walked straight past her cousin's army to safety.

Although Matilda controlled much of the south west of the country while Stephen was king, she never became queen of England. However, when her cousin died in 1154, he was succeeded by Matilda's eldest son, who became King Henry II/ the second.

Matilda returned to Rouen in Normandy in 1148, where she was known for being very religious, working with the Church and founding monasteries. She died in 1167 and is buried in Rouen Cathedral.

Find the right word(s) in the text above for each of the clues below:

1. The legal right to have or own something

_____

2. Stopped something from happening

3. Groups of people from the same country fight against each other in this (2 words)

4. A large group of soldiers who are trained to fight on land

5. Monks live in these places

6. Moved downwards

7. Taken prisoner

8. Get away from a place (that it wasn't possible to leave before)

9. The opposite of lightly

10. The opposite of danger

11. The opposite of life

12. A ceremony in which someone is crowned and becomes the king or queen of a country

13. The position of king or queen, or the large, ceremonial chair they sit on

14. Used weapons or force against a person or a place

15. A title given to the most important Catholic king in Europe (3 words)

/ 15

7. Richard III

Richard III / the third was only king of England for two years, but he is one of the most famous. This is partly because historians still can't agree whether he ordered the murder of his young nephews so he could become king. It is also, however, because he was the last English king to die in a battle, William Shakespeare wrote a play about him, and as a result of something extraordinary that happened in 2012.

Richard was the younger brother of King Edward IV / the fourth. When the king died after a short illness in April 1483, Richard was supposed to protect Edward's young sons, who were twelve and nine years old at the time. The older prince became king after his father, but his uncle may have prevented him from being crowned so he could be king instead. Richard arranged for the boys to stay in the Tower of London, a large castle next to the River Thames, but did he want them to be imprisoned and murdered, or protected? Once they were in the Tower, a law was passed by Parliament which made their parents' marriage illegal. It was claimed their father, King Edward, was already in a legal agreement to marry another woman before he married their mother. As a result of the law, the boys lost any right to the throne, and Richard became the new king in July 1483. The young princes were never seen in public again. Their disappearance and their uncle's actions made people think he had arranged their murder.

Richard and a distant cousin called Henry Tudor were both descended from King Edward III / the third, who had died more than a century earlier in 1377. Henry also believed he had a right to be king. In August 1485 he led an army against Richard and won the Battle of Bosworth Field. Richard was killed in the battle and for hundreds of years no-one knew where he was buried. In 2012 a skeleton was found under a car park in the city of Leicester. Experts examined it very carefully and a DNA test confirmed that it was Richard's.

Find the right word(s) in the text above for each of the clues below:

1. The bones of a human being connected together

2. A chemical in people, animals and plants that gives us genetic information

3. A large group of soldiers who are trained to fight

4. Make sure someone is safe and not hurt

5. The position of king or queen, or the large, ceremonial chair they sat on

6. The legal relationship between a husband and wife

7. Against the law

8. Well known

9. The crime of killing someone on purpose

10. This is normally performed in a theatre

11. Planned and organised something in advance

12. A verb used to say the body of a dead person was put in the ground

13. Told someone to do something or said it had to happen

14. A fight between two armies during a war

15. Have the same opinion about something

/ 15

8. Henry VIII

King Henry VIII / the eighth, who ruled England from 1509 to 1547, had six wives. His first wife was Catherine of Aragon, who was Spanish. After twenty-four years of marriage Henry wanted to divorce Catherine, but as a Catholic he wasn't allowed to, so he decided to change his country's religion instead. England became a Protestant country and, as a Protestant, he was able to divorce his wife. The pope in Rome was unhappy about this and punished Henry by saying he could no longer be a member of the Church.

Henry wanted to have a son to become king after him. Catherine had a baby boy but he died when he was two months old. His next wife, Anne Boleyn, gave birth to a daughter, (who later became Elizabeth I / the first), but didn't have a son. After a period of time, Henry thought Anne was seeing younger men. He became jealous and arranged for Anne to be executed. He then married Jane Seymour. She had a son (who later became the next king, Edward VI / the sixth), but Jane died only two weeks after he was born. His fourth wife was Anne of Cleves. A famous painter called Hans Holbein showed Henry a painting of Anne. She looked beautiful in the painting and Henry wanted to meet her. Although they got married, they didn't stay together because he soon decided he preferred a seventeen-year-old girl called Catherine Howard. Catherine became his fifth wife, but before long she was also accused of having sex with another man, and she suffered the same fate as Anne Boleyn. Henry's sixth and last wife, Catherine Parr, lived longer than he did. She was lucky.

Find the right word(s) in the text above for each of the clues below:

1. Feeling angry or unhappy because someone you like
   is showing an interest in someone else

2. The belief that God exists and all the activities and ceremonies related to
   the belief

3. Meeting someone regularly as a boyfriend or a girlfriend

4. Killed as a punishment for committing a crime

5. Controlled and had authority over a country

6. End a marriage legally

7. A picture made with oils or water colours

8. The legal relationship between a husband and a wife

9. The head of the Roman Catholic Church (2 words)

10. Made to suffer because they have done something wrong or broken the law

11. Permitted

12. Liked one person, (or thing), more than another

13. Let someone see something by putting it in front of them

14. Planned and organised something in advance

15. Fortunate

/ 15

9. Samuel Pepys

Samuel Pepys, (pronounced 'peeps'), was a member of parliament who also had the job of administering the English navy in the second half of the 17th century. For almost ten years between 1660 and 1669 he kept a diary, which is the main reason he is famous now. In his diary he wrote about his own personal experiences, but he also wrote about some of the great national events he witnessed, including the Great Plague. In London in 1665 about 100,000 people became ill and died because of a disease spread by fleas that lived on rats. The cause of the plague wasn't understood at the time, and a large number of dogs and cats were killed because people thought they were infected with the disease and were spreading it to human beings.

Pepys also wrote about the Great Fire of London. Early in the morning on the 2nd of September 1666 a servant woke him up to tell him about the fire, which had started at a bakery near London Bridge, and was spreading west. He went to the Tower of London to get a good view and then decided to take a boat onto the River Thames. From the river he could see houses burning and people desperately trying to remove possessions from their homes. Pepys wrote in his diary that he went to tell the king as soon as he realised how serious the situation was. It's not known how many people died in the disaster, but more than 13,000 houses were burnt / burned down and many of London's historic buildings were damaged or destroyed, including St. Paul's Cathedral.

Find the right word(s) in the text above for each of the clues below:

1. An unexpected event, such as a fire or a flood, that causes death and destruction

2. Had harmful bacteria in their bodies

3. Managing and organising a company or organisation

4. Very small, wingless insects that jump, and bite humans and animals

5. Damaged so badly that something no longer exists

6. Changed physically so something is broken or in worse condition

7. This was a prison for hundreds of years but now it's a famous tourist attraction (4 words)

8. Animals that look like very big mice

9. This is where people write down what they have done every day or what they plan to do in the future

10. A person who works in a house and does the cleaning, cooking or other jobs

11. Saw something and was able to describe it to other people

12. What someone can see from a particular place or position

13. The flames and smoke produced when something burns

14. Moved from one place to a larger area, or from a few people to a large number of people

15. The things people do or that happen to them in life

/ 15

10. The Industrial Revolution

In Britain, for more than a hundred years after 1750, there was so much change that the period is known as the Industrial Revolution. During this period, transport and communications improved greatly. Thousands of miles of roads and canals were built, and the first railway lines began to be used in the late 1820s. People moved to the towns and cities in large numbers to work in factories. In 1750 only 15% of the population lived in towns, but by 1900 the number had risen to 85%.

There were many inventions during the Industrial Revolution including photography, the bicycle, the phone and the motor car. In the early years, machines were invented for making things, and better techniques were used in the factories. Steam engines, for example, replaced water and horse power in many different industries. For this reason, factories could be built anywhere for the first time. It became much easier and faster to produce textiles, iron, steel and coal, which led to a huge increase in production. New and better ways of farming were also introduced and between 1700 and 1850 production on farms almost doubled. As a result of these changes Britain became a great trading nation. There were important changes in education too. A number of laws in the 1800s made education available and free to all children, including those from the poorest families.

Find the right word(s) in the text above for each of the clues below:

1. A hot gas which can be used to operate engines and machines. It comes from boiling water

2. The parts of machines that produce the power needed to make them work

3. Created, produced or designed for the first time

4. All the types of cloth produced in factories

5. The opposite of 'the richest' (2 words)

6. Methods and ways of giving or sending information

7. Ways of doing something which often require special skills

8. Trains travel on these (2 words)

9. A metal which is very hard and strong and is used to make steel

10. A metal that's used to make cars, ships, trains and planes

11. Buildings where goods are made

12. Man-made waterways

13. A hard, black object found underground and used to produce heat

14. Buying and selling goods

15. Teaching, training and learning

/ 15

ENGLISH LITERATURE

11. Geoffrey Chaucer

Known as the father of English literature, Geoffrey Chaucer was one of the greatest poets of the Middle Ages, a period in European history from the 5th to the 15th centuries. He lived from about 1343 to 1400, a time when most literature was in French or Latin, and his work helped English become accepted as an official, written language. Chaucer included approximately 2000 English words in his work that were used in spoken English, but had never been seen in written books or documents. Words we use in English, such as 'absent, accident, box, desk, finally, princess, scissors, theatre' and 'village', all appeared for the first time in Chaucer's writings.

Chaucer had a number of different jobs during his life. He was, of course, a writer, but he was also a philosopher, an astronomer, a messenger, a soldier, an administrator, and a diplomat, who represented his country abroad. He worked for important people, including the king of England, and other people worked for him. His life experiences must have helped him to write his poetry, and in particular, his greatest work, The Canterbury Tales. Telling stories was a popular form of entertainment in the 14th century. In The Canterbury Tales, a group of pilgrims tell stories to each other as they travel together on a journey from London to Canterbury Cathedral. There are more than twenty stories, most of which were written in verse by Chaucer, but some of them are in prose. There's great variety in both the story tellers, who are in very different jobs and positions in society, and in the stories themselves. The stories are interesting, amusing, and full of good and bad characters, who do good and bad things.

Find the right word(s) in the text above for each of the clues below:

1.   A tool used for cutting paper and cloth

2.   Stories, music, films, plays or books intended to please, interest or amuse people

3.   Someone who studies the planets in space

4.   Novels, plays and poems are all examples of this

5. The writing in novels rather than poems

6. The writing in poems rather than novels

7. This is where plays are performed

8. A person who works in an office may sit at this

9. A person whose job is to give written or spoken information to other people

10. In foreign countries

11. Religious people who travel to religious places

12. A person who studies the meaning of life, the universe and human beings

13. People in books, plays or films

14. Pieces of paper or books that give information about something

15. Chaucer was best known for being one of these

/ 15

12. William Shakespeare

One of the greatest writers in the English language was William Shakespeare, who lived from about 1563 to 1616. During his life he wrote more than 150 sonnets, which are poems that rhyme, have fourteen lines, and ten syllables in each line. He also wrote at least 37 plays, many of which were first performed on stage by actors at the Globe and Blackfriars theatres in London. His plays, which are mainly comedies, histories and tragedies, have become so popular that they are now read and studied by millions of people, and performed in theatres all over the world.

As You Like It, The Comedy of Errors, and Twelfth Night are three of Shakespeare's comedy plays. In his comedies, many of the characters make mistakes, often to do with mistaken identity, or misunderstanding what is happening. Other characters, including members of the same family, argue with each other, but in the end there's happiness and joy, with two or more people getting married.

Shakespeare's histories are mostly about English kings called Henry and Richard, who ruled between the 13th and 16th centuries, and a civil war known as the Wars of the Roses. He also wrote Roman plays about Coriolanus, Julius Caesar, and Antony and Cleopatra. All of these plays were based on the lives of real people in history, and many are tragedies, very sad stories with unhappy endings, as well as histories. This is because the main characters find themselves in bad situations or do things which cause them to lose everything they have, including their lives. Romeo and Juliet, Hamlet, and King Lear, are all main characters in three of Shakespeare's best-known tragedies.

Find the right word(s) in the text above for each of the clues below:

1. A word with the same meaning as 'errors'

2. A situation in which we think we know who someone is, but we're wrong (2 words)

3. Battles between two armies from the same country are fought during this (2 words)

4. Make something happen, which may be bad or unpleasant

5. People who play characters on stage, on television, or in films

6. The main sounds in words. There are five of these in 'misunderstanding'

7. Plays are performed in these places

8. A situation in which something is not understood correctly

9. Plays or films that are intended to be amusing or funny

10. An adjective with a similar meaning to 'unhappy'

11. Where the actors perform in a theatre

12. Periods of a hundred years

13. Controlled and had authority over a country and its people

14. Have a disagreement and speak angrily to each other

15. A verb used for words at the end of two or more lines of poetry, which have the same sound

/ 15

13. Charles Dickens

When Charles Dickens was still a young boy, his father lost his job and had serious problems with money. He was eventually arrested for debt and sent to prison, and before long other members of the family also left home and joined his father in prison. Dickens went to work in a factory so he could pay his rent and help his family. It was a very hard and boring job putting labels on pots ten hours a day. During this period of his life, he worked and lived in parts of London which were dirty, overcrowded, and full of poverty, rats and disease.

Dickens wrote fifteen novels between 1836 and 1870, when he died. No doubt his early experience in London helped him create the wonderful stories and characters in his books. He described in detail the city, its outskirts, the River Thames, and the places people lived and stayed in when they were travelling. He wrote about terrible working conditions, child labour in the factories, poverty, debt and crime.

Dickens' novels are full of secrets and surprises. His characters are of all ages and backgrounds; children and adults, rich and poor, good and bad. Some of them are very strange, others have amusing names, and the stories are about their relationships and what happens to them. There's love and rejection, and married couples who are not suited to each other. There are characters who marry to improve their social status, older men with younger women, husbands who are good to their wives, and others who are not. Some are kind and generous, others are mean or corrupt. Some treat children well and others are cruel to them. There are people who do bad things in Dickens' stories, and many of his characters have difficult lives, but good people normally find happiness or success in the end.

Find the right word(s) in the text above for each of the clues below:

1. An adjective for people who use their power or position to do dishonest things for money

2. The circumstances or situations which people work in (2 words)

3. A building that goods are made or manufactured in

4. Being told you're not loved, or accepted, by someone you love

5. Owing money to someone

6. Too many people in one place

7. The state of being poor or having very little money

8. Certainly true (2 words)

9. Where people have come from, especially their family, education, experience and class

10. Position in society in relation to other people (2 words)

11. Become or make something better than before

12. Unusual, surprising, or difficult to understand

13. Right for each other, or likely to be

14. Long stories with events and characters created by the writer

15. A place where people are kept as punishment for a crime

/ 15

14. George Orwell

Eric Blair was a novelist and journalist who used the pen name George Orwell. At different times in his life he was a policeman, a teacher, a soldier in the Spanish civil war, and employed by the BBC. He was born in India in 1903 but spent most of his life in England. Much of his work was influenced by his strong political views. In particular, he was opposed to totalitarian states with only one political party which had complete control and power over society. He disliked the idea that such a party should control all aspects of life, including the economy, education, and the private and public lives of its people. Orwell is best known for two novels which express these thoughts and feelings; Animal Farm, and Nineteen Eighty-Four.

In Animal Farm, which was published in 1945, pigs, horses, other animals and humans, are the main characters. It is thought to be based on the Russian Revolution, the rise of Stalin and Hitler, and a totalitarian government which eventually turns against its own people. In Nineteen Eighty-Four, he describes an unpleasant future world where the regime has total control over everything, even controlling how people think. Written in 1949, the book includes words and terms, for the first time, that have become part of our language. Big Brother, for example, is the dictator who watches what everyone is doing, and the Thought Police use force to stop anyone with opinions different from those of the regime. Orwell may even have been the first to use the expression, The Cold War, which described the USA's and the Soviet Union's relationship in the second half of the 20th century. These two novels, which he wrote not long before he died in 1950, are easy to read and very popular. George Orwell believed in using clear and simple English. One of his rules was that a long word should never be used "where a short one will do".

Find the right word(s) in the text above for each of the clues below:

1. A noun used for a government that hasn't been elected in a fair or democratic way

2. What writers use if they don't use their real names (2 words)

3. Disagreed strongly with something and wanted to stop it

4. Use actions or words to show what someone feels or thinks

5. This noun has a similar meaning to 'views'

6. The ability to make someone or something do what you want

7. A ruler with complete power over a country and its people

8. An adjective used for a country with only one political party which has complete control over its people

9. A writer whose news stories are in newspapers, online, on TV or on the radio

10. Violent, physical action

11. Stops being friendly to (2 words)

12. What can and can't be done, for example, in using a language

13. Battles between two armies from the same country are fought during this (2 words)

14. Enjoyed or liked by a large number of people

15. Affected and informed by (2 words)

/ 15

15. JK Rowling

JK Rowling was born in 1965 and started writing when she was six years old. One day in 1990, she was on a crowded train from Manchester to London, when she suddenly had the idea of Harry Potter, an idea that she soon developed into a story. The train had been delayed, and over a period of four hours, Rowling created the eleven-year-old boy who became the main character in seven novels that she wrote and named after him. She could picture him with black hair and glasses, an orphan who is amazed to discover he's a wizard in a world of non-magical people. The world of wizards exists in parallel with the real world and Harry Potter goes to a school called Hogwarts to learn the magical skills he needs to succeed there. He and the other students, including his friends, Ron and Hermione, also learn how to cope with the problems faced by teenagers, such as friendship, love and hate, studying, exams and becoming adults. Harry Potter uses his magical powers to defend himself and others against evil wizards, and his main enemy, Lord Voldemort, who killed his parents and wants to kill him. The novels and the eight films based on them are full of wonderful stories and characters. Children and adults all over the world have enjoyed them since the first book was published in 1997. Although she went on to write novels for adults using the pen name Robert Galbraith, JK Rowling is best known for her Harry Potter novels which have sold more copies than any other book series.

Find the right word(s) in the text above for each of the clues below:

1. Produced as a book or magazine and sold to the public

2. Manage or deal with something difficult

3. A person in a book, a play or a film

4. An adjective used for something amazing which doesn't seem possible in the real world

5. People with magical powers

6. What writers use if they don't use their real names (2 words)

7. A child whose parents have died

8. With and at the same time as (3 words)

9. An adjective used to describe a lot of people in one place

10. An adjective used to describe someone who is bad, cruel or enjoys hurting other people

11. A description of what people did, and what happened, invented by a writer

12. Particular abilities

13. Made late

14. A number of books, TV or radio programmes on the same subject with the same characters

15. These are made to be exactly the same as the others

/ 15

THE POWER OF SPEECH

16. Emmeline Pankhurst

Emmeline Pankhurst led the British suffragette movement in the early years of the 20th century. In 1903 she founded the Women's Social and Political Union, with the aim of getting women the right to vote in political elections. Although committed to direct action rather than words, early WSPU campaigns and meetings were mainly peaceful. However, as they continued to be ignored, the suffragettes became more militant. They damaged property, and met with opposition from the police, which often became violent. Many of them went on hunger strikes and were force-fed when they were sent repeatedly to prison. Their actions raised awareness of the injustice and inequality experienced by women in society and led to changes in the law in 1918 and 1928 which gave women the right to vote. In November 1913, Pankhurst gave a speech to an audience in the US which included these words:

"It has come to a battle between the women and the government...Now, I want to say to you who think women cannot succeed, we have brought the government of England to this position, that it has to face this alternative: either women are to be killed or women are to have the vote. I ask American men in this meeting, what would you say if....you were faced with that alternative, that you must either kill them or give them their citizenship? Well, there is only one answer...you must give those women the vote...I come to ask you to help win this fight. If we win it, this hardest of all fights, then, to be sure, in the future it is going to be made easier for women all over the world to win their fight when their time comes."

Find the right word(s) in the text above for each of the clues below:

1. An adjective used to describe people who use force or pressure for social or political change

2. These are arranged so people can get together and talk about or decide something

3. Planned activities intended to achieve a particular aim or objective

4. Again and again

5. A place that criminals serve their sentences in

6. A fight between armies, or a struggle to succeed in a difficult situation

7. Women who worked together to get women the vote

8. A formal talk that is given to, or in front of, a group of people

9. Protests in which people refuse to eat (2 words)

10. A noun used to say that people are not treated equally

11. People vote for someone in these political events

12. Choose someone or something in an election or a meeting

13. Buildings, land or possessions that are owned by people

14. Most difficult

15. A group of people who listen to words being spoken, or music being played

/ 15

17. Winston Churchill

Winston Churchill became British prime minister and leader of a wartime coalition government on the 10th of May 1940, at the age of 65. His appointment was unpopular with many MPs, but during the summer of 1940 he made a number of speeches in the House of Commons which won him the support and respect of politicians of all parties. The British public, and millions in the US and across the world, were also deeply affected by his radio broadcasts. They gave people belief and hope that Britain would defend itself against Adolf Hitler at a very dangerous and difficult time. When he spoke, he repeated a number of words to great effect, none more so than 'victory', (winning the war), and 'fight', (taking action to stop the enemy). Churchill's speeches inspired a nation, and encouraged its armed forces to carry on fighting until the 2nd World War ended in 1945.

"I have nothing to offer but blood, toil, tears, and sweat" he said on the 13th of May. "You ask, what is our aim? I can answer in one word: victory. Victory at all costs - victory in spite of all terror - victory, however long and hard the road may be, for without victory there is no survival." Then, on the 4th of June, just before the Battle of Britain, he spoke again in the House of Commons. "We shall go on to the end, we shall fight in France, we shall fight on the seas and oceans, we shall fight with growing confidence and growing strength in the air, we shall defend our island, whatever the cost may be, we shall fight on the beaches, we shall fight on the landing grounds, we shall fight in the fields and in the streets, we shall fight in the hills; we shall never surrender..." On the 20th of August, as British air force pilots were fighting in the air above Britain, Churchill spoke about the importance of their actions. "The gratitude of every home in our island...goes out to the British airmen who...are turning the tide of the World War...Never in the field of human conflict was so much owed by so many to so few."

Find the right word(s) in the text above for each of the clues below:

1. The opposite of 'friend'

2. The opposite of 'safe'

3. A government of two or more political parties working together

4. Give in and stop fighting, so you're at the mercy of the enemy

5. Programmes that are transmitted on television or radio

6. Belief in someone or something

7. The formal action of giving someone a particular job

8. Difficult, unpleasant and tiring work

9. Perspiration

10. Drops of liquid that come out of someone's eyes when they cry

11. A desire to thank someone for something

12. Changing how successful or lucky something is (3 words)

13. Formal talks given to, or in front of, a group of people

14. The continuation of life or existence, in difficulty or danger

15. Protect against attack

/ 15

18. Martin Luther King

Martin Luther King Junior led the civil rights movement in the US in the 1950s and 60s. He was committed to nonviolent action and resistance, having been inspired by Mahatma Gandhi, and his own Christian beliefs as a Baptist minister. A civil rights activist, he organised and led campaigns for racial equality on behalf of African Americans, before going on to campaign against poverty and the Vietnam War. He was imprisoned many times, but his work raised awareness of inequality and injustice across the world. It also led to changes in US law which ended legal segregation. In 1964, aged 35, he became the youngest man to win the Nobel Prize for Peace. Despite this, his life was often in danger, and in 1968 he was assassinated by a gunman in Memphis, Tennessee. In the US, the third Monday every January is a national holiday in his honour. Schools, public buildings and more than 700 streets in cities and towns have been named after him.

In 1963, Martin Luther King, and others, organised and led a march on Washington for jobs and freedom. At the Lincoln memorial, in front of more than 200,000 people, he gave one of the greatest speeches of all time. Known as "I Have a Dream", it was seventeen minutes long, and included these words:

"I say to you today, my friends, so even though we face the difficulties of today and tomorrow. I still have a dream. It is a dream deeply rooted in the American dream. I have a dream that one day this nation will rise up and live out the true meaning of its creed. We hold these truths to be self-evident that all men are created equal. I have a dream that one day, on the red hills of Georgia, the sons of former slaves and the sons of former slave owners will be able to sit down together at the table of brotherhood... I have a dream that my four little children will one day live in a nation where they will not be judged by the colour of their skin, but by the content of their character. I have a dream today."

Find the right word(s) in the text above for each of the clues below:

1. Take part in, or lead, planned activities with a political aim

2. Country

3. The separation and different treatment of people

4. An organised walk by a large number of people as a protest, or to express their opinions

5. The state of being poor

6. The rights everyone has to be treated equally (2 words)

7. Was the leader of

8. Given the confidence or enthusiasm to do something well

9. Murdered because they were famous or important politically

10. Based on, or originating in (2 words)

11. Friendship and understanding between people

12. A trained religious leader in the Christian church

13. Opposition to something, and refusal to obey

14. People who are legally owned by someone, who they are forced to work for

15. Out of respect and admiration for him (3 words)

/ 15

19. Barbara Jordan

Barbara Jordan was a lawyer, Democratic politician, and a leader of the civil rights movement. In 1966 she became the first black woman to win a seat in the Texas Senate, and the first African American member of the Senate since 1883. In 1972 she was elected to Congress, the first woman to represent Texas in the House of Representatives in her own right. She is best known, though, for two important political speeches. In 1974 she made a televised speech supporting the impeachment of the American President, Richard Nixon. Two years later, she became the first African American woman to make the keynote speech at a Democratic National Convention, which included these words:

"We believe in equality for all and privileges for none...This is a belief that each American, regardless of background, has equal standing in the public forum. All of us. Because we believe this idea so firmly, we are an inclusive rather than an exclusive party...We believe that the government, which represents the authority of all the people, not just one interest group, but all the people, has an obligation actively to seek to remove those obstacles which would block individual achievement; obstacles emanating from race, sex, economic condition. The government must seek to remove them. We are a party of innovation. We do not reject our traditions, but are willing to adapt to changing circumstances, when change we must. We are willing to suffer the discomfort of change in order to achieve a better future. We have a positive vision of the future, founded on the belief that the gap between the promise and reality of America can one day finally be closed. We believe that."

Find the right word(s) in the text above for each of the clues below:

1. A very important speech, introducing a meeting and its subject

2. Another word for 'power'

3. Succeed in doing something

4. A noun used for a feeling of certainty about something, or that something is true

5. A person who is qualified to advise people about the law

6.   Things that make it difficult to do what is needed or wanted

7.   Experience physical or mental pain

8.   A requirement to do something

9.   The action of charging a senior politician with a serious crime

10. Special rights or advantages some people have and others don't

11. Because of her own effort and qualifications, not because of who she knew (4 words)

12. Take something away or get rid of it

13. The introduction of new ideas or ways of doing things

14. The space or distance between two things

15. Refuse to accept something

/ 15

20. Stephen Hawking

Stephen Hawking, who was born in 1942 and died in 2018, was a physicist, author, and researcher, best known for his work on the origins and development of the universe. He suffered from a serious illness for most of his life, but in spite of this he continued to work as a cosmologist, and a spokesperson and role model for disabled people. He and eleven others signed a charter on disability in 2000 which demanded human and civil rights for the world's 600 million disabled people. He was involved in many fundraising activities and gave numerous talks, lectures and interviews on disability. On the 29th of August 2012 at the opening ceremony of the Paralympic Games, he communicated these words to a worldwide audience:

"The Paralympic Games is also about transforming the perceptions of the world. We are all different. There is no such thing as a standard or run of the mill human being - but we share the same human spirit. What is important is that we have the ability to create. This creativity can take many forms - from physical achievements to theoretical physics. However difficult life may seem, there is always something you can do and succeed at." Soon afterwards, in September 2012, his interview with the BBC included these words: "People have come to realise that the disabled are normal people who just happen to have certain special difficulties... I believe science should do everything possible to prevent or cure disability. No-one wants to be disabled if it can be avoided. I was diagnosed with motor neurone disease at the age of 21... That I'm still alive at the age of 70 is due in large part to the excellent care I have received. It has also helped that I have been successful in my scientific career. This has kept me active and I travel a lot although I'm almost paralysed. I hope my example will give encouragement and hope to others in similar situations. Never give up."

Find the right word(s) in the text above for each of the clues below:

1. Unable to move all or part of the body

2. A meeting in which questions are asked to assess someone, or find out their opinions

3. A person people admire and want to copy (2 words)

4. A scientist who studies different types of energy and how they affect objects

5. Ordinary and not special in any way (4 words)

6. An illness in which the nerves and muscles gradually become weaker (3 words)

7. The ways people see and think about things

8. A scientist who studies the origins and development of the universe

9. Changing something completely

10. The imagination or ability needed to produce something new

11. All the jobs that someone has or does in their life

12. A written statement of the rights a group of people should have

13. Collecting money for a charity or other organisation

14. Had a particular illness or disease confirmed by a doctor

15. Support, courage, and hope

/ 15

21. British Politics

The United Kingdom, known as the UK, is a democracy and a monarchy, and a monarch, (a king or a queen), is the head of state. The prime minister is the head of government and leader of the political party which has won a general election. After the election, he or she chooses about twenty members of parliament, or MPs, from the party to become members of a powerful group called the Cabinet. Each of these senior politicians is in charge of a department. There are departments for every important area of government, including the economy, education, health, the environment, and transport.

In a general election, normally held every five years, candidates from different parties compete against each other to win a seat in the House of Commons and become an MP. To do this, a candidate has to get more votes than any other candidate in his or her local area, which is called a constituency. Once elected, the new MP represents all the people in his or her constituency in Parliament.

A party has to have a majority of MPs, or more than half of the 650 seats, to win the election and become the government. If no party manages to do this, the parties with the most seats try to gain a majority by going into an alliance, or coalition, with one of the other parties, so their combined number of seats, or MPs, is more than 325.

Find the right word(s) in the text above for each of the clues below:

1. An event in which the people vote for candidates to become members of parliament (2 words)

2. The government department responsible for schools and universities

3. Chosen to do a particular job because they got the most votes

4. Lorries, buses, cars, trains and planes

5. More than 50% of something

6. Exactly 50% of something

7. Someone who is in charge of a school, a government or the state

8. Politicians responsible for particular departments are members of this (2 words)

9. A political system in which people elect the politicians who govern their country

10. The person in charge of the British government (2 words)

11. An MP represents all of the people who live in this

12. A country with a political system and government

13. A verb used to say that someone acts or speaks on behalf of others

14. People choose a politician in an election by using these

15. Put together

/ 15

22. UK Political Parties

Since the 1920s, the two largest political parties in the UK have been the Conservatives and Labour. The Conservatives are sometimes called the Tory party and their members and supporters are known as Tories. Their policies have tended to be right-wing. They've tried to lower taxes and reduce public spending by making cuts to public services in the UK, which has included local government, health care and transport. The UK debt is billions of pounds, and a priority for the government has been to pay the money back over time.

The Labour Party is considered a left-wing party which has normally supported higher taxes and increased public spending. They've accused the Conservatives of helping rich people, London and the south of England and not doing enough to help poorer people in other parts of the country. The Scottish Nationalist Party, or SNP, the Liberal Democrats, and the Democratic Unionist Party of Northern Ireland, or DUP, are the three largest parties in the House of Commons after the Conservatives and Labour. In recent elections, the Liberal Democrats and the DUP, on separate occasions, have joined the Conservative party to form a coalition government. The Conservatives needed their MPs in order to gain a small majority in the House of Commons and become the government. In December 2019, however, the party won a general election with a large majority of 80 seats and, as a result, were able to govern on their own.

Find the right word(s) in the text above for each of the clues below:

1.   An expression used for socialist views and a belief in public ownership

2.   An expression used for capitalist views and a belief in private ownership for profit

3.   Plans of action chosen by political parties

4.   Money paid to a government so it can pay for public services

5.   More than 50%

6.   Money that someone owes and should be paid back

7.   A government provides these to help people (2 words)

8.   Reductions in the amounts of money spent on public services

9.   The Parliamentary body whose members are elected by the people (4 words)

10. Lorries, buses, cars, trains and planes

11. Using money to pay for public services (2 words)

12. The most important thing to do

13. A government with two or more political parties working together

14. The opposite of 'richer'

15. Thousands of millions

/ 15

23. The European Union

The European Union, known as the EU, is an economic and political union of 27 member states. It operates through a system of independent organisations, such as the European Parliament and the European Central Bank. It also operates with the help of European governments whose politicians have meetings, talk to each other and make decisions. As a result, the EU has developed a single market, and makes laws for all its member states. Some of these laws ensure the free movement of people, goods, services and money across borders in the EU. Others make it possible for countries to work together on crime and immigration and have common policies on trade, agriculture, fisheries and regional development. Regional development is intended to help countries do better business, improve their economies and create jobs. Climate change, energy supply and globalisation are all part of the policy too. Globalisation is to do with countries becoming more similar and connected to each other because of large international companies and the Internet.

Most EU countries have the same currency, the euro, although some countries use their own currency. The European Central Bank in Frankfurt, Germany, has policies for the euro, and in particular, keeping inflation under control. This means making sure the price of everything in the shops doesn't go up too quickly.

The UK joined the EU in 1973. On the 23rd of June 2016, after 43 years of membership, a referendum was held to decide whether the UK should remain in the EU. 52% of people who voted chose to leave, and 48% to remain. In a process that came to be known as Brexit, the UK ceased to be a member of the EU.

Find the right word(s) in the text above for each of the clues below:

1. An occasion when all the people in a country can vote on an important issue

2. The system of money that a country or a group of countries uses

3. The amount of money you have to pay to buy something

4. Farms and farming

5. Businesses that do something for customers or other people, but don't produce goods

6. Become better or make something better

7. The parts of the seas where fish are caught in large numbers

8. Travelling and moving to a new country to live there permanently

9. The lines, and land near the lines, that divide two countries

10. Legislation

11. Things that are produced and transported to be sold

12. The rise in prices of goods and services in a country

13. Providing power, such as oil, gas or electricity for heating and machines (2 words)

14. Actions that are against the law

15. Buying and selling between countries

/ 15

24. American Politics

The United States of America is a republic with a federal government. This means that each of the fifty states has control over its own political activities, but whenever national decisions are made, the states are controlled by central government in Washington DC. The constitution of the US divides the federal government into three branches to make sure no individual or group has too much power. These branches are the Legislature, (Congress), which makes the laws; the Executive, (the President, Vice President and the Cabinet), which ensures the laws are carried out or actioned; and the Judiciary, (the judges of the Supreme Court and the federal courts). The President, who's in charge of the Executive, (but isn't a member of Congress), is supposed to be advised by the Cabinet, which includes the heads of the executive departments and other senior government officials.

Congress consists of the Senate and the House of Representatives, known as the House. The Senate is smaller than the House, (there are two senators for every US state), but its members are more senior and include the Vice President. In the House, the number of representatives from each state is related to the size of its population. California has the largest population so it also has the largest number of representatives, which can be more than fifty. States with the smallest populations have only one representative.

There are both Democrat and Republican politicians in Congress. Democrats, who tend to be more left-wing, normally support higher taxes, more money for public services such as health care and education, and help for poor people. Republicans tend to be more right-wing and believe in the right to possess guns, and the death penalty. Their policies usually result in lower taxes, but less money for public services and increased military spending.

Find the right word(s) in the text above for each of the clues below:

1. Plans of action chosen by political parties

2. Weapons which fire bullets

3. A person, country or organisation that's part of a particular group

4. Money paid to the government so it can pay for public services

5. Money used for the army, navy and air force (2 words)

6. Rules in a country which tell people what they can and can't do

7. Politicians in the Senate

8. All the people who live in a particular city or country

9. The opposite of 'junior'

10. Medical treatment as part of a public service (2 words)

11. The punishment in some US states for very serious crimes (2 words)

12. An adjective used for people with capitalist beliefs

13. An adjective used for people with socialist beliefs

14. The laws and principles by which a country, or a state, is governed

15. A country governed by a president and politicians elected by its people

/ 15

25. Democracies and Elections

One of the best things about democracies is that people can choose and vote for the politicians they want in an election. We're very lucky not to live in a country ruled by a dictator, or where there is only one political party. Dictators believe they can do whatever they want. This includes using force against their own people, especially if there are protests or demonstrations against the dictator. Democracies are not perfect, but most people agree they're a better form of government than any alternative.

Before an election, opinion polls give people an idea of how popular the parties are. Each party tries to get as much publicity as possible so that the voters learn more about the party's candidates and their policies. Senior politicians and other party members travel round the country, going from door to door, meeting people and making speeches. There are party political broadcasts and adverts online and in newspapers. Party leaders take part in debates on television.

On polling day, in each constituency, people go to their local polling station to vote. They are given a piece of paper which has the names of the local candidates and their parties on it. They put a cross next to the name of the person and party they wish to vote for. Then they put their piece of paper in a container called a ballot box. At the end of the day, all the votes are counted and the candidate with more votes than any other candidate becomes the member of parliament for their local area.

Find the right word(s) in the text above for each of the clues below:

1. A district which elects its own member of parliament

2. A ruler who has complete power and control over a country

3. Surveys used to find out what people think (2 words)

4. Public actions to show that people oppose or disagree with something

5. Public actions to show that people support or are protesting against something

6. A formal word for the activity of voting

7. People who are trying to be elected, or are applying for jobs

8. Formal talks given to audiences

9. Something else you can choose if there are two or more possibilities

10. Violent action

11. Activity to get people to know about or pay attention to someone or something

12. Radio or television programmes

13. Information in the media intended to make us want a product or a service

14. Choose a candidate or a political party on polling day

15. Plans of action chosen by political parties or businesses

/ 15

26. The Welfare State

A welfare state is a country whose government makes sure its people receive the practical and financial help they need. In a welfare state there is less poverty than in countries without welfare. People have more opportunities and a fairer share of a country's wealth. Those earning a lot of money pay more tax than others who don't earn very much. People with no income, or very low incomes, pay no tax. In the UK, the money raised by these taxes goes towards the pensions and benefits that are given to people in need. They also pay for services such as health, which is provided by the National Health Service, and care and education provided by local government.

The welfare state in the UK was created between 1906 and 1914, when pensions, free school meals, health care, and financial support for people who were unemployed, all became available. This was followed in 1942 by the Beveridge report, named after William Beveridge, an economist and social reformer. The report advised the government to provide enough income, health care, education, housing, and employment for people in need. By 1948 new laws had been introduced which resulted in the practical and financial help the Beveridge report had asked for.

Find the right word(s) in the text above for each of the clues below:

1. Work

2. Get or obtain money for working

3. The total amount of money a person receives a year

4. Payments people receive because they need financial help

5. The amount of money or property that a person or a country has

6. Gave recommendations and opinions on a particular situation

7.   Amounts of money paid to older people when they no longer work

8.   Teaching, training and learning

9.   Medical services provided for people (2 words)

10. More appropriate and just

11. The state of being poor

12. A person whose work results in social or political change

13. Not having a job, or not working

14. Accommodation, or places for people to live

15. Chances to do something or achieve something

/ 15

27. Local Government

In the UK, the national government is responsible for running the country. Local government deals with towns, the areas around them, and parts of cities. In London there are 32 local governments which are called councils. The income tax that people pay goes to the national government who then give some of it to the councils. The councils use this money to pay for the services they provide. There is a separate tax, called council tax, that people pay directly to their local council, which also pays for local services. The amount of council tax paid is related to the value of each person's home, so people who own expensive properties pay more than people who own cheaper ones.

Once they receive the money, which is more than twelve billion pounds a year in total, the councils spend it on different services which are intended to help local people and their families in their everyday lives. These include education, the emergency services, leisure, housing, waste, and social services. Social services departments are responsible for the care and support of disabled and elderly people, as well as children and adults at risk. The other services provided by the councils are parking, libraries, the environment, transport, roads, and planning. Planning departments deal with applications, for example, to replace a door or a window, build an extension, or change a building into flats. The health service, or NHS, (which is short for the National Health Service), is not provided by local councils, but almost everything else is.

Find the right word(s) in the text above for each of the clues below:

1. Activities, including sports, that people do in their free time

2. Materials that are no longer needed and are thrown away or recycled

3. The natural world and all the people, animals and plants that live in it (2 words)

4. In charge of a nation, an organisation or a business, and managing it

5. Another word for 'old' that we use to describe people

6. An adjective used for people with a physical or mental impairment who are unable to do certain things

7. Ambulance workers, the police and fire fighters (3 words)

8. In danger of being harmed or hurt (2 words)

9. Most people who earn money have to pay this to the government (2 words)

10. Most people who own a flat or a house have to pay this to their local authority (2 words)

11. How much something is worth

12. These are provided by councils for local people

13. Flats and houses

14. A new room, (or rooms), which is added to a house

15. Connected with (2 words)

/ 15

28. Disability
....

Disability is a word used to describe a physical or a mental impairment that may prevent some people from doing things other people are able to do. For many disabled people, it's caused by a part of the body which doesn't function. Other disabled people have lost a part of the body in an accident, a war or because of a disease. Disability can be inherited, happen during birth or while growing, or be caused by illness or injury.

The challenge for a caring society is to enable people with disabilities to live as full a life as possible. With modern technology it is now possible to do far more than it was hundreds of years ago. Wheelchairs and artificial limbs were in use by 1800, but they are now widely available and can improve the lives of more people with disabilities than ever before. Another important development has been a wide range of computer software which has made it easier for disabled people to communicate, work and socialise.

In 1948 doctors at a hospital in the UK began using sport to help injured soldiers. Since then, sport has been an important part of disabled people's lives because of its physical and psychological benefits. Millions of athletes with disabilities take part in sports every day. Many have competed in sports events like the Special Olympics, the Paralympic Games and the Invictus Games. Disabled people in sport, and in life, are showing the world what can be achieved.

Find the right word(s) in the text above for each of the clues below:

1. Disabled people who are unable to walk use these

2. This word has a similar meaning to 'before' and 'in the past'

3. The Paralympic and Olympic Games, and the football World Cup are all examples of these (2 words)

4. An adjective which has a similar meaning to 'mental'

5. An adjective related to the body

6. An adjective used to say you can buy, get or find something

7. Being kind to other people and helping them

8. Physically hurt

9. Work in the correct way

10. Arms and legs

11. Stop someone from doing something

12. A noun which has a similar meaning to 'disability'

13. Received something from their parents

14. A new or difficult task that tests what people can do

15. Not real

/ 15

29. Care for the Elderly

Although many people continue to be active, happy and well in later life, old age increases the chance of longer-term medical conditions and problems. Elderly people are more likely to suffer from frailty, dementia, disability, illness, and dependence. Much can be done for many of these people to enable them to carry on living at home, and being independent, and in some cases, elderly people are cared for and looked after by a member of the family. Other people, however, move into care homes when it is no longer safe for them to live at home, they can no longer look after themselves, or they choose to do so.

In the UK, charities and the social services departments of local councils also offer a range of services. These make it possible for people to continue living in their own homes, and special equipment such as stairlifts can be installed in their houses. There are carers who help elderly people get up in the morning, wash and get dressed. They visit some of them during the day and help them go to bed in the evening. Many also do the shopping for people who are unable to do it themselves. Others make sure elderly people have hot meals brought to their homes when they have stopped cooking for themselves.

Loneliness is a problem for many elderly people. They feel lonely because they live alone and no longer see, or spend time with, the people they knew when they were younger. Charities and councils try to help by arranging for them to join groups and take part in daytime activities. Much more could be done, however, to deal with the situation, including more regular visits from neighbours and members of the family. The challenge for a caring society is to make sure elderly people are not on their own, live as full a life as possible, and receive the care that they need.

Find the right word(s) in the text above for each of the clues below:

1. Weakness and poor health

2. People who take care of sick, disabled or elderly people

3. Chairs that take people up to the first floor, or down to the ground floor, of their homes

4. An adjective that has the same meaning as 'elderly'

5. A physical or mental impairment which stops a part of the body functioning

6. Put clothes on (2 words)

7. Unhappy because someone has few or no friends and feels alone

8. The state of needing the help and support of other people

9. Things people do for achievement, enjoyment or interest

10. Fixed into place so it can be used

11. A mental condition which causes memory loss and difficulty with thinking

12. Elderly people who don't live at home are looked after in these places (2 words)

13. Feeling and being healthy

14. Make it possible for someone to do something

15. Councils help people in need and so do these other organisations

/ 15

30. Education, Health, and Benefits

In a welfare state, taxes are paid to a government and the government uses the money to pay for services and benefits. Two of the main services are education and health care.

There are private schools in the UK, but most schools are state schools. Private schools can be very expensive, but state schools are free, which means that parents don't have to pay for their children's education. There are private hospitals in the UK, too, but the National Health Service, or the NHS as it is known, provides free health care for everyone who needs treatment. Someone with a medical problem can go to see a doctor who is called a GP, (short for general practitioner), and they don't have to pay for the service. If someone needs to go to hospital and stay there for a period of time, this is free as well.

There are also benefits, which are payments provided by the government for people who need financial help. For people who are out of work and can't find a job there's unemployment benefit. For men and women who have reached retirement age there's a state pension. There are payments for disabled people and for carers who look after other people. Income support is for people on low incomes, and housing benefit helps people on low incomes to pay their rent. Many of the other benefits are related to children. There's maternity benefit, an adoption payment, and for families on low incomes there's child benefit. All of these benefits are intended to help people in need.

Find the right word(s) in the text above for each of the clues below:

1. Money paid to a woman who is having a baby (2 words)

2. Money paid to a person who doesn't have a job (2 words)

3. Money paid to the legal parents of someone else's biological child (2 words)

4. Money paid to an older person who no longer works

5. Money paid by a tenant to a landlord every month

6. Money paid to people who don't earn very much (2 words)

7. These provide children with free education (2 words)

8. The opposite of 'long'

9. The stage in life when someone has stopped working

10. A verb with the same meaning as 'arrived at' or 'got to'

11. Medical help given to a patient with a particular illness or injury

12. Medical help and support provided by the NHS and other organisations (2 words)

13. The opposite of 'cheap'

14. A country in which practical or financial help is given by the government to people in need (2 words)

15. An adjective used for people with an impairment which prevents a part of the body from functioning

/ 15

31. Colds and Flu
....

When you're working or studying it's important that you feel well so that you can do your best. There are some very common illnesses that affect more of us in the winter than at other times of year. If you get a cold, (you can also say catch a cold), you'll have a number of symptoms. A cold often starts in your head and makes you feel tired and unwell. A day or two after this the cold normally spreads to your nose and throat, before it moves to your chest. You'll probably need some tissues to wipe your nose. You may sneeze a lot and have a sore throat. Colds tend to last a few days or a week but some can last for months. This is because they're caused by more than 200 viruses and some of these make us ill for longer than others.

You don't usually have to stay in bed if you have a cold. Most people carry on with their normal lives even if they don't feel very well. If you get (or catch) flu, though, you'll probably feel much worse and won't feel able to study or work during the day. With flu, (the long word is 'influenza'), you could have a headache or a fever, which is when your temperature rises, or chills, which is when you feel very cold. You may feel hot and cold at different times. You'll also have some or all of the cold symptoms I've mentioned. Both colds and flu are very infectious so try not to go near other people. If you have flu, the most sensible thing to do is to go to bed and rest until you feel better.

Find the right word(s) in the text above for each of the clues below:

1. Flu is the common name for this illness

2. This word means the same as 'painful'

3. Goes up

4. A sore throat, sneezing and headaches are all examples of these

5. A verb used to say we are in one place for a period of time

6. Another way of saying 'continue' (2 words)

7. Tiny living things, too small to see, that infect people, animals and plants

8. If your head feels painful for a while, this is probably what you've got

9. An adjective used to describe an illness that one person can give to another person

10. A noun used to say how hot or cold our bodies are, or the weather is!

11. A verb used to say something moves from one place to other places

12. The part of your body used to swallow food and water, or other drinks

13. This happens suddenly and you can't control it!

14. The top part of the front of the body between the neck and the stomach

15. A medical condition in which the temperature of the body is higher than normal

/ 15

32. Diseases in Poor Countries

There are many diseases in the world that are related to poverty. People are still very poor in some countries. As a result, they suffer from malnutrition. They become ill because they don't have enough food to eat, or are eating the wrong food. In many cases they don't have clean water either. Clean water is needed for people to drink. It's needed when people wash themselves, too, and when they wash their clothes. It's also needed for cooking. Without it, diseases spread quickly, especially in crowded, dirty living conditions.

In parts of Africa, there are three very serious diseases which kill people every day: malaria, tuberculosis, or TB, and HIV AIDS. In these places there isn't enough health education or health care. This means people don't know about the dangers or can't avoid them. What makes everything worse is that most of them won't get the right medical help when they're sick.

It's common for people to have both malaria and HIV at the same time. When this happens their HIV virus is much stronger, so they infect other people more easily. People with HIV, or who suffer from malnutrition, can become ill with TB. This is because their immune systems are low. In Africa, more people with HIV lose their lives because of TB than anything else. If there's malnutrition, dirty water, and disease all in one place, more men, women, and children are likely to become sick and die. It's a tragic situation.

Find the right word(s) in the text above for each of the clues below:

1. The opposite of 'right'

2. A service that teaches people how to stay well and not become sick (2 words)

3. Another way of saying people 'die' (3 words)

4. The opposite of clean

5. The state of being poor, or having little or no money

6. A service that looks after people and gives them medical help (2 words)

7. The short form of this infectious disease is TB

8. Another word used to say someone is ill or has an illness

9. An adverb that means the same as 'fast'

10. Mosquitoes carry this disease and infect people with it

11. A word used to say that people give a disease to other people

12. These help our bodies to fight infections and diseases and stay healthy (2 words)

13. An adjective used to say a lot of people are in the same place at the same time

14. Another word for illnesses which make us sick

15. An adjective used to say how sad it is that people are dying or have died

/ 15

33. Diseases in Rich Countries

Many of the diseases people suffer from in rich countries are related to how we live. We choose a particular lifestyle because we enjoy it and can afford it. It's easy and fun to drive everywhere, so we stop walking. We've got TVs, computers and mobile phones, so we spend our evenings and weekends at home instead of going out. During the week many of us go to school, or work, and sit at a desk all day. There's less time to take exercise.

We can choose what we like to eat or drink, but so much of what we choose is bad for us. Food with a lot of fat in it, or sugar, or both. We put salt in our cooking and on our plates. We don't eat enough fruit and vegetables. Many of us still smoke cigarettes as well, and we drink too much alcohol.

It's a lifestyle that can cause problems later in life. A lack of exercise, poor diet, being overweight, smoking, and drinking, can all result in a number of serious illnesses. One of the most serious is cancer. There are many different types of cancer. Some forms of the illness can be cured, but people still die of other forms unless they are diagnosed early. Other serious illnesses are heart disease and strokes. People with heart disease are in danger of dying from heart attacks. If someone has a stroke, a blood vessel in the brain becomes blocked, or there's bleeding, and this can also be fatal. It's not all bad news, though. We're much less likely to die of these illnesses if we change our lifestyles!

Find the right word(s) in the text above for each of the clues below:

1. This word has the same meaning as 'kinds' or 'types'

2. An adjective which means something causes or results in death

3. A piece of furniture in a classroom or an office

4. A serious disease which can be in different parts of the body

5. Heavier and fatter than we should be if we want to be healthy

6. This disease and cancer are two of the most serious (2 words)

7. The food that we eat and the drinks we drink

8. Treated so someone recovers from an illness and is healthy again

9. Physical activity that people do to be healthy or become fitter

10. Sudden serious illnesses in people's brains

11. A substance in meat, cheese and other food which is bad for us if we have too much of it

12. Some of us put this on our cereal and in our tea and coffee

13. These happen when people's hearts suddenly stop working (2 words)

14. A word used to say a doctor has found out what someone's illness is

15. A thin tube that carries blood through our bodies (2 words)

/ 15

34. Doctors and Chemists

If you're not feeling well, or you've got an ache in a part of your body, what do you do? If you don't think it's serious, you could go to your local chemist and get something to treat it. The chemist, who sells medicines, (and almost anything you might need in your bathroom), may be able to help, but if not, they normally advise you to see a doctor. There should be a surgery near you where there are doctors who can examine you to see what the problem is. You will need to contact the surgery and register with them. Once you've registered you can ask for an appointment. When you go to your appointment, which may be a few days later, the doctor will diagnose the problem and help you get the right treatment. If it's a problem which is easy to treat, they may tell you to go back to your chemist and buy some tablets or a cream over the counter. But if you need a strong medicine, the doctor will write you a prescription. This is a piece of paper which has information on it about the medicine you need that you take with you to the chemist. The chemist reads the prescription and lets you know how long it will take to prepare the medication your doctor has prescribed.

Your doctor may not be sure what your medical problem is, in which case you would normally be referred to see a specialist. This means they arrange for you to see a doctor with a lot of medical knowledge of the part of the body or the illness that you're worried about.

Find the right word(s) in the text above for each of the clues below:

1. The shop assistant or chemist stands on one side of this and the customer stands on the other side

2. Small, round pieces of medicine that you swallow with water

3. Unhappy and afraid because of a problem

4. A place where doctors or dentists see their patients

5. The opposite of 'weak'

6. A chemist won't sell you a strong medicine without this

7. Find out exactly what an illness or a medical problem is

8. A pain that you could have in your head, back, stomach or even a tooth

9. Practical help with a particular medical problem

10. An arrangement to meet or visit a doctor or a dentist at a particular time and place

11. Sent to another doctor

12. Put your name and personal details on a form when you contact or go to a surgery for the first time

13. A person who is an expert in a particular area of work or study

14. Information, skills and understanding someone has gained from education and experience

15. Look closely at someone or something to find out what's wrong

/ 15

35. Hospitals

In the UK, when someone has an accident and gets injured, or feels very sick, they may have to call 999 and ask for an ambulance to take them to hospital. The ambulance reaches them as soon as it can, and a paramedic might have to give the casualty some medical treatment before they set off. If they don't need an ambulance, most people who are injured or sick are driven to hospital by a friend or relative or take themselves. When they arrive, they go to the A&E department which stands for Accident and Emergency. They wait there for their turn to see a doctor who decides what treatment is needed. People who have treatment and go home the same day are known as outpatients. Other people who stay in hospital overnight or for several days or weeks are called inpatients. Hospitals have a number of departments for different types of injury or sickness, such as burns and cuts, cancer and heart disease. There's normally a maternity department as well, and for very serious injuries or illnesses there's an intensive care unit. Most departments have rooms called wards and there are beds in each ward for inpatients. People who have medical insurance may have a private bedroom and can normally choose to go to a private hospital. In the UK, however, most large hospitals are part of the NHS, or National Health Service, and are public hospitals.

Find the right word(s) in the text above for each of the clues below:

1. This could be from the evening until the following morning

2. Large rooms which have beds in them for inpatients

3. The continuous care and attention given to seriously ill patients (2 words)

4. An ambulance worker who treats casualties but isn't a doctor

5. Women who are going to have babies are in this department or ward

6. A member of the family

7. Medicine or other medical help given to a patient

8. When someone is suddenly hurt or injured and no-one did it on purpose

9. This means 'is the short form of' (2 words)

10. Start a journey to another place (2 words)

11. A person who is injured in an accident

12. These injuries are caused by fire

13. These injuries happen when skin is broken and there's bleeding

14. More people in the UK die from this serious illness than any other illness

15. Expensive medical treatment may be paid for by the company you have this arrangement with (2 words)

/ 15

36. Crime
....

If someone does something wrong and breaks the law, we say a crime has been committed. Different words are used in the English language for different crimes and the people who commit them. A murderer commits a murder and a rapist is guilty of rape. Terrorists cause terrorism and hijackers hijack planes or cars. Muggers mug people, burglars burgle houses and robbers rob shops, post offices or banks. Arsonists commit arson. For people who lose their lives or suffer physical or psychological harm as a result of serious crimes, and for their families, these are terrible events. Most of us, however, only find out about the worst offences when they're reported in the news, because as terrible as they are, they are still relatively infrequent.

There are other crimes that are more common, though. Do whatever you can to avoid becoming the victim of a crime. When you're in the street make sure any valuables you're carrying, such as money and mobile phones, are hidden from view and can't be stolen from your bag. Be very careful with personal or financial information, online banking and any passwords or pin numbers. Don't buy drugs from a drug dealer. You can never be sure what you're buying and they could make you ill or even kill you. Never get into a car with a driver who's been drinking alcohol or taking drugs. You're much more likely to be in a car accident if you do. If you're driving, or a pedestrian, or a cyclist, look out for dangerous drivers too. Dangerous driving is a crime and people die on our roads every day because motorists are careless or drive too fast.

Find the right word(s) in the text above for each of the clues below:

1. People who start fires on purpose

2. People who use violence for political, religious or other purposes

3. Very unpleasant or causing great harm or injury

4. A person who sells illegal drugs (2 words)

5. Put or kept in a place where it can't be seen

6. People who break into houses or flats and steal things

7. People who go into shops or banks and steal things

8. A person who uses force or violence to have sex with someone

9. A person who kills someone on purpose

10. Taken from another person without permission or any intention of giving it back

11. People who attack other people in public places to steal their money

12. People who use violence or threats to take control of a plane or a car

13. A person who's had something stolen, or been attacked, injured or killed in a crime

14. Small personal things that are worth a lot of money

15. An adjective which means 'bad', used with nouns like 'problem, crime, illness' and 'damage'

/ 15

37. Emergencies

An accident or a crime can become an emergency. In an emergency someone who witnesses what's happened calls the emergency services by dialling 999 and asks for the ambulance, the fire service, or the police. In a situation where one of the emergency services needed is the police, police officers on foot or in police cars go as fast as possible to the scene of the incident. If someone has been injured, an ambulance drives to the scene and a fire engine may go to put out a fire. These vehicles all have sirens and flashing lights so people can hear them, see them, and move out of their way to let them go past.

When the emergency services arrive, they often find people who are upset, angry, or frightened. Anyone who is hurt or injured is usually treated in the ambulance by a paramedic and taken to hospital. If the police think someone may have caused an accident or committed a crime, they talk to the people involved, and any witnesses, asking questions about what they saw or did. After talking to them, a suspect may be arrested if it's believed a crime has been committed, or they disobey a police officer. In some cases, often when people become violent, the police put handcuffs on them before taking them to the police station. At the police station someone who's committed a serious offence is normally charged and placed in custody. In the event that a crime is considered less serious, and it's thought the offender is unlikely to reoffend or cause any problems, bail may be granted, and the person is released until they are due to stand trial.

Find the right word(s) in the text above for each of the clues below:

1. Formally accused of committing a crime

2. An adjective used to describe someone who is trying to hurt or kill another person

3. This describes a bright light which goes on and off continuously

4. Refuse to do, or will not do, what a person tells you to do

5. Two metal rings joined by a chain which are put round someone's wrists

6. A sudden, serious and dangerous event or situation which requires urgent action to deal with it

7. Pressing the numbers on a phone to make a call

8. This person isn't a doctor but is trained to help people who are injured or hurt

9. If this is given, someone charged with a crime can pay money to be free until they have to go to court

10. A bad event that no-one intended to happen and may result in injury or damage

11. Another noun which means the same as 'crime', (an action which breaks the law or is illegal)

12. Taken to a police station and kept there for a period of time because the police believe the person has committed a crime

13. Sees something happen and may later have to describe what they saw

14. These make loud noises to warn people about a fast-moving vehicle

15. In prison for a period of time before going to court (2 words)

/ 15

38. The Police

In the UK, the police have a lot of different jobs to do. They take turns to work day and night shifts so there are police officers on duty 24 hours a day. The police attend demonstrations and sports events to make sure they are peaceful, but when we see them in our cities and towns they are normally 'on patrol'. This means police officers in uniform drive or walk around the area they work in. When they're on foot, they speak to people in the community and find out what's happening. This gives them important information about the local area and it reassures people that they are there to help and protect them. Anyone who sees them and is thinking of committing a crime is less likely to go ahead with it because they realise they may get caught.

Another responsibility for the police is to respond to calls from the public about crimes and accidents. They speak to, and support, the victims of crime and witnesses, collecting evidence and taking statements. They also carry out investigations using the latest technology or traditional methods. Part of an investigation may be to search people, property, vehicles or land. It's not all exciting detective work, though. They have to do a lot of administration when they get back to the police station because all the information has to be recorded and put in a report.

Find the right word(s) in the text above for each of the clues below:

1. People who see something and may have to describe it later

2. Information that makes us believe something is true. The police may look for it at the scene of a crime

3. Written down and kept so it can be used whenever needed afterwards

4. A piece of writing which gives the facts and says what happened in a particular event or situation

5. Walking (2 words)

6. People who have suffered or died in an accident, crime or because of a disease

7. Police officers, soldiers or nurses while they are working (2 words)

8. Periods of time during which a group of people work until they're replaced by other people

9. Public meetings or marches at which people support or protest against someone or something

10. Official examinations of crimes, events or situations to find out the truth

11. Clothes which are the same, worn by everyone in a particular group or organisation

12. Sherlock Holmes did this kind of work!

13. All the people who live in a particular area

14. Descriptions given by witnesses and other people which are written down by police

15. Look carefully for something

/ 15

39. The Courts

A person who is charged with a criminal offence in the UK may be given bail, which means they can go home until they have to attend court and face a legal trial. For more serious offences, such as murder, rape and robbery, bail is not normally permitted. The person charged is kept in custody until the hearing, and when the trial takes place, it's held in a Crown Court. Someone being tried in court is referred to as the accused.

A trial is a formal examination of evidence by a judge and a jury. The judge is in charge and controls what happens in court, and the jury, twelve men and women who are members of the public, listen to everything said during the trial. They listen to the judge, experienced lawyers known as barristers, and any witnesses or other people who are asked to speak. One of the barristers defends the accused by arguing that they haven't committed a crime and are therefore innocent. The other barrister prosecutes the accused by arguing that they have committed a crime and are guilty. When the jury have considered what they've heard, they make their decision, which is called reaching a verdict. If they conclude they're guilty, the accused is convicted and the judge announces what punishment is to be given. If the jury believe they're innocent, the accused is acquitted, and the judge states officially in court that they can go free.

Find the right word(s) in the text above for each of the clues below:

1. An action which is against the law and has a similar meaning to 'offence'

2. People who saw a crime happen and are asked in court to say what they saw

3. Allowed

4. Giving reasons to persuade a jury that the accused is innocent or guilty

5. The crime of killing someone on purpose

6. Using force or violence to have sex with someone against their will

7. Using threats or violence to steal money or goods from a shop or a bank

8. In prison until someone goes to court (2 words)

9. Found guilty of a crime at the end of a trial

10. Found innocent of a crime at the end of a trial

11. A court (in England and Wales) that deals with serious criminal cases (2 words)

12. The facts that make you believe something is true or untrue

13. Speaks on behalf of the accused in a trial

14. Tries to prove that someone in court is guilty of a crime

15. A close look at something (to see if anything's wrong, or there's a problem)

/ 15

40. Punishment and Prison

People who are charged with a crime have to go to court to be tried. If the accused is found guilty, the judge decides and then says what the punishment will be, which is called passing sentence. About three quarters of all sentences in the UK are fines, which are often for driving offences or theft. The amount of the fine depends on how much someone can pay and the seriousness of the crime, but it could be hundreds or thousands of pounds in some cases. If the accused is considered a danger to the public, or for more serious crimes, they are usually sent to prison for a period of time, and those guilty of murder can expect a 'life sentence', which means they'll be there for many years. In the UK, unlike some other countries, there is no death sentence. The death sentence for murder was abolished in 1965.

For less serious crimes, the punishment could be a suspended sentence. This is known as being put on probation. It means criminals won't go to prison if they behave well and don't reoffend. They also have to attend regular meetings with a probation officer for a period of time. Another punishment for less serious crimes is community service. Community service is unpaid work which is done in the local area to help local people. The judge in court decides how long the community service should be.

There are more people in prison in the UK than at any time in the past, and about 95% of them are men. Many of these prisoners are behind bars either for a long time or a very short time. About 20% of prisoners are serving a life sentence, but almost 50% are in prison for six months or less.

Find the right word(s) in the text above for each of the clues below:

1. The place where a legal trial takes place

2. This punishment means a person would go to prison if they reoffend during their probation period (2 words)

3. An amount of money that must be paid as a punishment for committing a crime

4. This punishment means a person found guilty in court will lose their life (2 words)

5. The crime of stealing

6. The person who controls what happens in court and decides on the punishment

7. To be at an event, such as a trial, a class or a meeting

8. Punishments given by a court

9. The opposite of 'innocent'

10. This informal expression means that a person is in prison (2 words)

11. An adjective used with nouns like problem, crime, offence and illness

12. Commit another crime

13. Formally accused of a crime

14. A verb used to say how people conduct themselves, and whether they do this well or badly

15. This adjective means that no money is received for doing something

/ 15

WORDS AND NUMBERS

41. English Grammar

Students who learn English spend much of their time studying English grammar. There are rules in English and all other languages which help us understand how to change the form of words, and put words into the right order in sentences so they are grammatically correct. There are eight different types of word in the English language which all have a different function in a sentence and are called parts of speech. In alphabetical order, these are adjectives, adverbs, conjunctions, determiners, nouns, prepositions, pronouns and verbs. Teachers explain English grammar to students and give them examples and exercises when they have understood the rules. Before students start their English course and attend their lessons, they normally buy a dictionary and at least one grammar book, unless they decide to access all these resources online. Students who don't know which books to choose, or where to find the information they need online, should talk to their teacher, or the person who has helped them register. People working at the school should be able to advise students what resources are recommended or most suitable for the course they're about to start.

Find the right word(s) in the text above for each of the clues below:

1. 'In, from' and 'to' are three examples of these parts of speech

2. Parts of speech which add information to verbs and adjectives. Many of them end -ly or -lly

3. A word used to say what something does or how it works

4. These tell us what we can and can't do with words in English

5. Parts of speech which join words, phrases or sentences; 'and', 'but' and 'or' are three examples of them

6. This word means 'right for a particular occasion, event, purpose or situation'

7. Parts of speech used for actions and states

8. Parts of speech used for people, animals, places and things

9. There's a capital letter at the start of the first word and a full stop after the last word of these

10. This means the same as 'sorts' and 'kinds'

11. These short words are used instead of nouns.

12. The eight different types of word with different functions (3 words)

13. Parts of speech that describe people, places or things and usually go before nouns

14. You do this when you join a school and your name is put on the list of students

15. The articles 'a', 'an' and 'the'

/ 15

42. English Vocabulary

If English grammar is about changing words and putting them into the right place in a sentence, English vocabulary is about the meaning of words. It's about the meaning of all the words we use when we speak and write the English language. It takes time to learn a language, mainly because there are so many words to learn. A good question to ask is what we need to do to learn these words. Of course, it's important to be able to pronounce them properly, but we will only be able to add them to our vocabulary when we learn and understand what they mean. English teachers help students understand words by explaining them in English, and giving students vocabulary exercises to do. A lot of these exercises are online and they're in vocabulary books too, which students can use at home or take to school. Whenever they don't know the meaning of a word, they should make sure they look the word up online or use a dictionary.

Find the right word(s) in the text above for each of the clues below:

1. This means the same as 'be certain' (2 words)

2. People who teach students

3. Know how something happens or what something means

4. Look a word up in a dictionary to learn this

5. Where someone is if they're in their apartment or house (2 words)

6. This word means doing something 'in the right way'

7. When we ask something, this is what we ask!

8. A book which has all the words in the language in alphabetical order, and gives the definition of each one

9. Questions in a book used to test or practise what someone knows

10. On the Internet

11. Make the sound of a word or a letter when we speak

12. The opposite of 'few'

13. This means the same as 'correct'

14. Telling someone about something in a way which makes it easy to understand

15. We usually read these either because we enjoy them, or because we're studying them

/ 15

43. Words for Feelings

During our lives we experience a lot of different feelings and emotions. In the English language, words called adjectives are used to describe these emotions. People feel happy or sad, optimistic or pessimistic, proud or ashamed. When we have strong positive emotions, we are often very pleased or delighted, but if we experience strong negative emotions, we may feel angry or upset.

Some adjectives have two different endings. Adjectives which end -ed tell us how someone feels, but the same adjectives which end -ing say how someone or something is. So, for example, I was interested in watching a football match on TV because it should have been interesting, but nobody scored a goal. I got bored, (this was how I felt), because the match was boring, (how it was). I changed channels and started watching a film, but within minutes I was frightened. It was a frightening scene. Then I became terrified, because the film had become terrifying. I switched over again to the news, but started to feel depressed because the news was depressing. I was getting annoyed and irritated as well. The remote control wasn't working properly, which was annoying and irritating. I decided to go to bed because I was tired after a tiring week at work. Then the phone rang. It was a friend who sounded very excited and had some exciting news. He'd been offered a job he really wanted, but he seemed so surprised. I asked him why it was surprising. He explained that something embarrassing happened at the interview, which made him feel very embarrassed. Someone brought him a cup of tea and he knocked it over. The tea went all over the table, the floor and the wall. He was so disappointed. He'd convinced himself he wouldn't get the job, which was terribly disappointing for him. When he told me what happened, though, I couldn't stop laughing. I was very amused because the story was so amusing!

Find the right word(s) in the text above for each of the clues below:

1. The opposite of boring, but less exciting than exciting!

2. This word has a similar meaning to 'funny'

3. Something isn't as good or successful as you'd hoped

4. A word with a similar meaning to irritating

5. Very frightening

6. Embarrassed and / or upset because of something you've done, or someone else has done

7. Very pleased

8. Feeling you need or want to sleep or rest

9. Scared or afraid

10. Feel shy or awkward in a difficult situation, often in front of other people

11. Having no interest in what you're doing, or nothing to do

12. Expect bad things to happen in the future

13. Expect good things to happen in the future

14. Feeling pleased and enjoying life

15. Pleased with what you've done, someone you know, or something you own

/ 15

44. Numbers and Calculations

When we want to talk about amounts or quantities we use numbers. For instance there are 75 centilitres of wine in a bottle, 31 days in March, and 52 cards in a pack. For large numbers which end with less than a hundred, the word 'and' is said before the number at the end. Using the number 23 as an example, we say one hundred and twenty-three and would also say one thousand and twenty-three, and one million and twenty-three! We do this with any combination of millions, thousands and hundreds. To give you an example of this, I've chosen two million, four thousand, one hundred and ten, which written as a number is 2,004,110. When we write numbers, they're written without any words, but there are commas after millions and thousands.

For years such as those in the first decade of the century, we tend to say two thousand and one up to two thousand and nine. After that, though, it's common for us to say the first two numbers and then the second two numbers, so twenty ten and twenty eleven, right up to twenty ninety-nine. If we were to write the years I've mentioned in this paragraph as numbers, we would write 2001, 2009, 2010, 2011 and 2099. No commas are used for years written as numbers.

Calculators on mobile phones make it easier to do calculations anywhere and anytime / any time. In the English language there are different words for each of the main types of calculation. These are 'addition, subtraction, multiplication' and 'division'. The words that are often used, though, for each type of calculation are: 'plus, minus, times,' and 'divided by'. On phones and keyboards, symbols are used instead of words. These symbols are: + - x and /, and the word 'equals' written as a symbol is =.

Find the right word(s) or numbers in the text above for each of the clues below:

1. Ten years

2. 'cl' is an abbreviation of this word

3. A short word often used when numbers are multiplied

4. The number of weeks in a calendar year

5. Is the same in quantity, size or value as something else

6. Two or more things mixed or joined together

7. An adjective used for anything which is done frequently, happens often, or exists in large numbers

8. Things that process numbers to find out a total amount or quantity

9. Three quarters of a hundred

10. A fifth of a hundred and fifteen, expressed as a number, not a word

11. A hundred years

12. These may have clubs, diamonds, hearts or spades on them

13. A sign, number or letter that has a meaning in maths or science

14. A verb used to say that we usually do something, or how something normally is

15. The opposite of 'more difficult'

/ 15

45. Shapes and Sizes

If you want to describe an object, like a table or a window, you may need to mention its shape. Some of the most common shapes are rectangles, squares, triangles and circles. Half a circle is a semi-circle. These words are all nouns, but if you're thinking about a particular object it's possible to use the adjectives, most of which are the same as the nouns except for the endings. You might, for instance, talk about a rectangular table, a square window, slices of pizza which are triangular, or describe wheels or roundabouts as circular or round.

There are many different ways of describing sizes, depending on what something is, as well as how small or how large it is. We use words for animals, objects and places, such as small, medium-sized or large. The smallest of these could be described as tiny, and the largest as enormous or huge. Clothes are small, medium, large or extra-large, and the same adjectives are used for eggs in supermarkets, except the largest are 'very large'. We also use numbers for clothes, including measurements for the collar, chest, waist and legs, and sizes for dresses, socks and shoes. In the UK, if you want files, envelopes or pieces of paper that are the right size, it's useful to know whether you need A3 for the large ones, A4 for medium size ones, or A5 for smaller ones. Whenever you look for something online, or in a shop, there are usually words, letters or numbers, or a combination of these, to help you find what you want.

Find the right word(s) in the text above for each of the clues below:

1. We go round in these if we're not achieving anything

2. Pieces of food that have been cut off a larger piece

3. The part of a shirt which goes round the neck

4. A synonym of the word 'enormous'

5. Shapes with three straight sides

6. Shapes with four straight sides that are the same length

7. Shapes with four straight sides, two of which are longer than the other two

8. Traffic goes round these

9. A square and a circle are two examples of this

10. You need these if you want to know the size or length of anything

11. A belt is worn around this part of the body

12. Not too large and not too small (3 words)

13. Bicycles have two of these and most cars have four

14. Say or write something, but with little information

15. Very or extremely small

/ 15

SCIENCE

46. Biology

Biology is a science about things which are alive. In particular, it's about all the animals and plants on our planet. Many have similar features which enable us to put them into groups, such as class, order, family, genus and species. By doing this, animals and plants can be identified more easily and students can learn about them.

Biology students learn how animals and plants can only exist with the right habitats and ecosystems to support them. They are taught how life starts with reproduction, how genes are passed on to the next generation, and the role of DNA. They study the impact of hormones on growth, and how cells prevent disease by receiving and sending signals. They learn how nerves respond to touch, temperature, light and sound.

Biology is also about nutrition, digestion and excretion and how they are essential to life. These are all about what goes into the body, how it's broken down inside and then how it leaves the body. Respiration and breathing are essential too, as are gases such as oxygen, carbon dioxide and hydrogen, and how they are used. In animals, blood transports everything needed around a circulation system. In plants, water is moved from the roots to the leaves, and food is carried from the leaves to the rest of the plant. Whatever's required, nature finds a way of providing it, and biology is a way of learning about it.

Find the right word(s) in the text above for each of the clues below:

1. Capital letters used for a chemical in the cells of animals
   and plants that carries genetic information

2. The parts of a plant which are below the earth. (The first letter is 'r')

3. A physical process by which air moves in and out of the lungs. (b)

4. This is below family and above species in the classification of animals and plants. (g)

5. A more formal word for breathing. (r)

92

6.   Places where particular types of animal or plant are normally found. (h)

7.   Interactions of animals and plants with each other and their physical environment. (e)

8.   A process by which living things get the food they need to grow and be healthy. (n)

9.   Genes are found inside these tiny units of living matter. (c)

10. The production of babies, young animals or plants. (r)

11. We get these from our parents which is why we are like them. (g)

12. How food is changed into substances the body can use. (d)

13. The movement of blood around the body. (c)

14. Chemicals produced in the body that help us to grow. (h)

15. These carry messages between parts of the body and the brain. (n)

/ 15

47. Chemistry

Chemistry is the study of matter, which is really everything in the universe. Matter exists in different forms: solids, liquids, gases and plasma. It only changes when it's made to change by some outside force. If you add energy, such as heat, to a solid, it can become a liquid, and more energy can turn it into a gas. With a lot more heat, a gas changes to plasma. These changes from solids to plasma are all about groups of tiny things called atoms, which break away from each other and move further and further apart.

Everything around us is made up of atoms, so they're everywhere, but far too small for us to see them with our eyes. Inside every atom there are what could be described as dots of electricity called protons and neutrons, which are joined together. Amazingly, there are even smaller, lighter particles called electrons that move round them and are part of the atom. Atoms with the same number of protons are called elements, and two or more elements joined together form a compound. These elements and compounds, in turn, form substances, and either pure substances or a mixture of pure substances form matter.

Chemists study chemical reactions in substances. They want to know how substances react under different conditions. They're interested in what happens when they're combined or in contact with each other. There are organic chemists, who study carbon and its compounds, and there are inorganic chemists, who study almost everything else. The polymer, petrochemical and pharmaceutical industries all depend on organic chemists. There are millions of organic compounds, and more are invented or discovered every year, so these chemists are busy people!

Find the right word(s) in the text above for each of the clues below:

1. A chemical element found in all living things. (The word begins with 'c')

2. An adjective that goes before compounds, chemists, and food with no artificial chemicals. (o)

3. Water is one of these. (l)

4. Hydrogen is one of these. (g)

5. A type of energy we use for lighting, heating, and driving machines. (e)

6. An adjective which means very small, or extremely small. (t)

7. Space and everything in it, such as planets and stars. (u)

8. This industry produces oil and gas. (p)

9. This industry produces plastic. (p)

10. This industry produces drugs for medical use. (p)

11. Tiny round marks, like full stops in punctuation. (d)

12. An adjective used for chemists whose work is about substances that don't contain carbon. (i)

13. Chemical changes when two or more substances act on each other. (r)

14. Created something that hadn't existed before. (i)

15. Found something that no-one had found before. (d)

/ 15

48. Physics

Physics is the scientific study of energy and matter, and the interaction between them. It's the study of forces such as heat, light and sound, the relationships between them and how they affect objects. A force causes an object to change, and unbalanced forces cause changes in direction, shape or speed. The way everything moves, rises and falls, accelerates or slows down, can be explained by physics.

We rely on energy in everything we do. There's energy in moving objects, and potential energy in objects that aren't moving. There's energy in heat, light and sound, and in fuel, food and batteries. There are many forms of electrical energy as well. Electricity can be generated from fossil fuels and nuclear power, although it's non-renewable energy. It can also be generated from wind, water, geothermal and solar energy, and these are renewable forms of energy. We rely on electromagnetic energy every time we switch on a light, or turn it off. There's even energy stored in stretched or squashed objects.

Waves are also sources of energy, and they're used in many different ways. We only have to think of the waves in the sea to understand how much power and energy they can generate. They're used for TV and radio signals, for microwave ovens and mobile phones, for x-rays and radiotherapy in hospitals, and of course, light waves make it possible for us to see. Sunlight is a mixture of electromagnetic waves, or radiation, from the sun. Physics is extraordinary. It explains much of what happens on Earth and answers many questions about the universe as well.

Find the right word(s) in the text above for each of the clues below:

1. An adjective used for the natural heat of rock in the ground. (The word begins with 'g')

2. These actions change the movement of objects, often by pulling or pushing them. (f)

3. Pressed or squeezed, so it becomes flat, or changes shape. (s)

4. Moves faster. (a)

5. Space and everything in it. (u)

6. This adjective means 'from the sun'. (s)

7. An object that has been lifted or raised has this type of energy. (p)

8. Metal, with electricity going through it, that attracts other metal. (e)

9. Coal, oil or gas formed millions of years ago from dead animals and plants (2 words).

10. Power that comes from the protons and neutrons in atoms. (n)

11. How fast something moves. (s)

12. A circle, a square, or a triangle. (s)

13. Food can be cooked very quickly in these. (2 words)

14. Can be replaced naturally and won't all be used. (r)

15. These produce electricity and can make things work. (b)

/ 15

49. Maths

The most common type of maths, which is the short form of the word 'mathematics', is arithmetic. Arithmetic is the operation of numbers in addition, subtraction, multiplication and division. Two or more numbers can be added, subtracted, multiplied or divided, and each calculation gives us a result. 'Plus, minus, times' and 'into' are other words which we use for these operations, and we put the word 'equals' before the number that we've calculated. All four operations and the word 'equals' are also represented by symbols, which are used much more than words in written calculations.

Other types of maths are taught in schools and universities, such as algebra, geometry, statistics, probability and calculus. In algebra, letters and symbols are used to represent quantities, whereas geometry is to do with the measurements and relationships of lines, angles, surfaces and solids. Statistics is all about information shown in numbers which give us a better idea of what is happening in a particular situation. Probability, often expressed in percentages, is about the future and the chances that something will happen, and calculus deals with rates of change, for instance, in a population over a period of time, or the speed of a moving object from the start to the end of its movement.

Find the right word(s) in the text above for each of the clues below:

1. How much or how little things change, for example, over time or distance (The word begins with 'r')

2. The word we use for the symbol = (e)

3. These can be straight, curved, dotted, parallel or wiggly, as well as horizontal, vertical or diagonal. (l)

4. We use 'times' or the symbol x for this operation. (m)

5. We use 'into..' or the symbol / for this operation. (d)

6. We use 'plus' or the symbol + for this operation. (a)

7. We use 'minus' or the symbol - for this operation. (s)

8. These can be represented by the symbol % . (p)

9. The spaces, measured in degrees, between lines or surfaces that are joined together. (a)

10. The amounts or numbers of things. (q)

11. Signs, numbers or letters that represent or mean something. (s)

12. You need these if you want to know the size or length of anything. (m)

13. The actions of using numbers to find out how much or how many of something there are. (c)

14. All the people who live in a particular city or country. (p)

15. Walls, floors and ceilings are all examples of these (s)

/ 15

50. Computing

Whenever we use a computer, we give it a set of instructions, which is known as input. The computer then processes the input and produces a result, which is called output. On a PC, normal input is done by typing on a keyboard and clicking with a mouse, but using a camera and a scanner are other ways of doing it. On phones and tablets, input is carried out simply by touching the screen. The instructions then go to a microprocessor, which is the part of the computer that contains all the functions of the central processing unit, or CPU. It's here that the information is processed. Once it's been processed, the output on a PC is usually shown on a screen, but output can also be sounds from speakers or a printed document from a printer. There are very different outputs from different computers.

Computers have both hardware and software. Computer hardware is all the physical parts of a computer that we can actually touch. We know about some of these parts, such as the computer case, monitor, keyboard and mouse. Other parts, though, are inside the case, so can only be seen if the computer is opened up. There's a plastic board, called the motherboard, which has the CPU and the main memory on it. There's also a hard disk drive which stores all the data files and software applications, and an optical disk drive to read and write information. Unlike hardware, software can't be touched. It's all the computer programs that control the hardware and operate the computer. Software is translated into codes which the hardware can understand and process. Hardware and software are both essential to a computer. One couldn't work without the other.

Find the right word(s) in the text above for each of the clues below:

1. We use this to take photos. (The first letter of the word is 'c')

2. These are written so a computer can perform specific tasks (2 words)

3. This is moved across a mat to position a cursor on a screen. It's also a small mammal! (m)

4. The container or outside of a computer. (c)

5. We hear these when they reach our ears. (s)

6. This is where data is stored for future use in a computer. (m)

7. This is where information on disks is read and stored (d)

8. This copies pictures and documents so they're stored in a computer. (s)

9. We press the keys on this to enter data into a computer. (k)

10. Another word for a screen on a computer. (m)

11. These computers are larger than smartphones but smaller than PCs. (t)

12. Instructions changed into machine language that the computer understands. (c)

13. Information which tells a person or a computer what to do. (i)

14. Carries out operations on data in a computer. (p)

15. The parts of a computer that the sound comes out of. (s)

/ 15

HUMAN BEINGS

51. How We Think

One of the main differences between human beings and all other forms of life is our highly developed brain. In the early stages of development, we competed with other mammals and reptiles for food, and relied on our instincts to find enough to eat and stay alive. This started to change when we learnt to walk on two legs, and use our hands to do things. At the same time our brains grew larger and more intelligent. We became conscious of ourselves and our actions, and adapted to our environment.

Unlike animals, human beings have become creative, productive, and resourceful. Our brains are capable of abstract thought, reasoning and planning. We have feelings and memories, and think about time, life and death, and right and wrong. Our use of language has enabled us to communicate and understand each other. We have personality, humour, and self-control, and appreciate beauty and pleasure. With these extraordinary developments, human beings have become the most advanced and powerful creatures on the planet. With power, though, comes responsibility. All of us, and in particular our governments, have a responsibility, to protect life, the environment, and the world we live in.

Find the right word(s) in the text above for each of the clues below:

1. Our ability to laugh at things and find them amusing

2. Crocodiles and snakes

3. The personal qualities and character that make someone different, interesting or attractive

4. Human beings, tigers, lions, dogs and cats

5. Thinking about things in a logical way

6. These are inside our heads. They control our feelings, memories, movements and thoughts

7. Feelings that make us react or do something without thinking or using reason

8. The opposite of late

9. Changed something to make it more suitable for a new situation or environment

10. Based on ideas and not on anything real (2 words)

11. Depended

12. Enjoyment

13. Thoughts about the past

14. Having a duty to do something

15. Having the ability to produce something new

/ 15

52. How We Look

Identical twins look very similar, but most other people look different from each other. Our skin colour is so varied that no two individuals are the same. People are tall, short or medium height. There are thin or slim people, and others who are normal weight, or overweight. A healthy diet and regular exercise help us look fit and well. An unhealthy lifestyle, though, can make us look unfit and unwell.

Some people are thought to be good-looking or attractive. Good-looking women are frequently described as beautiful, girls as pretty, and men or boys as handsome. The negative tends to be used to say the opposite, so for example, that someone isn't good-looking.

People's hair is so different that we often mention it before anything else. Hair is naturally straight, curly or wavy. Some of us have short or medium length hair, and others grow their hair until it's long. The word for men who are losing their hair is 'balding', and men with little or no hair are bald. Hair can be a number of different colours, but most people in the world have black or brown hair. The rest have red, ginger or yellow hair, and someone with yellow hair is often described as blonde / blond. When people get older, their hair normally goes grey, and in many cases turns white. There's a wide variety of different hairstyles as well, and the choice of a centre parting, a side parting or a fringe. For people with long hair, a ponytail, bun or plaits are options. Finally, although a lot of men shave every day, others grow stubble, or have a beard or a moustache. With so many possibilities, no wonder we all look different!

Find the right word(s) in the text above for each of the clues below:

1. Healthy, strong, and in good physical condition because of regular exercise

2. Very short hairs that grow on a man's face when he doesn't shave

3. Hair that grows on a man's chin and cheeks if he doesn't shave for a long time

4. Hair that grows between a man's nose and his top lip

5. A positive word or a compliment for someone who is thin

6. An adjective used for hair which is curved

7. An adjective used for lots of small rings of hair on someone's head

8. The same or almost the same

9. An adjective used for people who are heavier or weigh more than normal

10. The line on someone's head where their hair is divided by a comb or a brush

11. This colour is a mixture of brown and orange

12. How people grow, arrange, or have their hair cut

13. An adjective used to describe people whose height is greater than average

14. The food we eat and the drinks we drink.

15. Long pieces of hair divided into three parts and twisted together

/ 15

53. How We Move

Human beings move around in different ways, so there are words in the English language for all the types of movement. Dancers dance, climbers climb and swimmers swim. Babies crawl and soldiers march. In most situations, children and adults walk from one place to another, but if we're in a hurry we sometimes run. Sports players jump to reach a ball, or a net, and athletes take part in the high jump, the long jump and the triple jump. When we visit a town or a city for the first time, many of us like to take a stroll and wander round. Whenever we go for a walk, though, it's important to take care and watch where we're going. If we don't, we could trip over something, and when there's ice or there are wet leaves on the ground, it's easy to slip and fall. Anyone who falls and hurts a foot or a leg might not be able to walk normally. When this happens, they may walk with a limp.

We move other parts of our bodies even when we're not walking. We stretch our arms and legs when we get up in the morning, or before exercise. When we're sitting, we often cross our legs or fold our arms. We turn our heads and shrug our shoulders. We wave with a hand, and point with a finger. We lean forwards, backwards or against a wall, bend our knees, pick something up, put it down, carry it somewhere, throw it or catch it. Sometimes our bodies move when we don't even want them to. We tremble with fear, shiver with cold, and jump when someone or something gives us a shock!

Find the right word(s) in the text above for each of the clues below:

1. Move or bend our bodies so they are no longer vertical

2. Shake when we're frightened

3. Push ourselves upwards and off the ground

4. Go up a mountain, a hill or a tree

5. Shake because it's freezing!

6. Move something so it faces a different direction

7.   Move through water using our arms and legs

8.   Move around on our hands and knees

9.   A slow, relaxed walk

10. Move slowly around a place without going in a particular direction

11. Raise and drop our shoulders to show we don't know or don't care
     about something

12. Someone who's injured a foot or a leg might walk with this

13. Walk with regular steps like people in an army

14. Drop from a higher level to a lower level

15. How we move if we want to get somewhere quickly

/ 15

54. How We Sound

We use our voices to make sounds and communicate with other people. In most situations we talk or speak to someone. There are other sounds we make, though, whenever we experience and are affected by strong emotions or feelings. We laugh when something is funny or hilarious, and young children often giggle. We cry when we're very unhappy, happy or sad, or feel deep sympathy. We groan if we're annoyed, upset or in pain, and sigh with relief, sadness or frustration. We yawn when we're bored or tired, and puff and pant if we're exhausted and out of breath. We whisper to say something quietly, shout to say something loudly, and scream because we're furious, terrified or in agony.

The voice does other things too. It's used as a musical instrument, not only to sing, but also to hum and whistle. We intend to make these sounds, but there are other sounds we don't normally make on purpose. Anyone with a cold might sneeze or cough, babies burp, and we sometimes hiccup / hiccough again and again until we drink some water. There's one sound, though, that we're almost always unaware of. When we're asleep some of us snore so loudly we wake other people up!

Find the right word(s) in the text above for each of the clues below:

1. Very frightened

2. Very amusing

3. Very tired

4. Very angry

5. The word for this sound rhymes with, (has the same sound as), 'off'

6. The word for this loud sound rhymes with 'ease'

7. The word for this sound rhymes with 'more'

8. The word for this sound rhymes with 'chirp'

9. The word for this extremely loud sound rhymes with 'theme'

10. Breathe quickly and loudly through the mouth after hard physical exercise (3 words)

11. Laugh in a silly way when you're amused, embarrassed or nervous

12. Make a tune with your lips closed

13. Make a tune with your lips closed except for a small round opening in the middle

14. A sound made when someone is in pain, upset or irritated

15. A sound made when someone is disappointed, sad or relieved

/ 15

55. Communication

We normally communicate by talking to people, but there are numerous forms of non-verbal communication too. For many of these we use our faces, or our faces give information to others. Most of the time we intend this to happen, but it's a form of communication that may not be intended, and we may not even be aware that it's happening! The expressions on our faces tell other people how we're feeling. When we're happy or amused, we smile with our mouths and with our eyes. We open our mouths and yawn when we're bored or tired, and may also open them if we're surprised or amazed. We blush when we're ashamed or embarrassed, and put our hands over our mouths when we're shocked or horrified.

We use our eyes in many different ways as well. If we feel very emotional, many of us cry, and tears come out of our eyes. We glance at something to check it and stare at someone or something if we're thinking about them. Have you ever used your eyes to wink at someone when you wanted to share a joke or a secret? Can you remember the last time you were dazzled by bright light, and it made you blink? How do you react when you're surprised ? Do you raise your eyebrows?

We frequently use gestures with our heads or our hands to give information to others. These gestures are also forms of non-verbal communication. We shake our heads to disagree with someone or say 'no', and nod to agree or say 'yes'. We raise a finger in front of our mouths when we want someone to be quiet. We clap and wave with our hands, point at something with a finger, and knock to let someone know we're at the door. In the UK, if we point a thumb upwards, it means that something's good or it's gone well. If we point it downwards, it means it's bad, or it's gone badly. A gesture could have a different meaning in another country, so be careful when you use them abroad!

Find the right word(s) in the text above for each of the clues below:

1.   A movement with our heads or hands which shows what we mean or want to say

2.   An adjective used for a silent form of communication

3.   Close and open one eye quickly

4.   Close and open both eyes quickly

5. Lift or move something upwards

6. Hit your hands together, often more than once

7. Humans have four fingers and this on each hand

8. Look at someone or something for a moment only

9. Look at someone or something for a long time

10. In a foreign country

11. Stretch out a finger to show where someone or something is

12. Lines of hair above each eye

13. Go red in the face

14. Raise one hand and move it from side to side to say 'hello' or 'goodbye', or to get someone's attention

15. The looks on people's faces which show their emotions

/ 15

56. Having a Baby

When a woman is pregnant it means she's going to have a baby. It's normally about nine months before she gives birth. Being pregnant can be a difficult time for a woman, and there's a lot to learn. Doctors and nurses at the local health centre are able to give advice. There are also ante-natal classes, and there's information online for women and their partners, which makes it easier for them. They learn about having a baby, and looking after it when it's very young and small. Most women suffer from morning sickness, which makes them feel sick, and in some cases vomit, in the early months of pregnancy. Although it's called morning sickness, women may be unwell at any time of day, but they normally feel better by the fourteenth week.

The period of time just before a woman gives birth is called labour. For a first baby, labour usually takes about eight hours, but it could be much shorter or longer. When a woman goes into labour, she needs to be taken to hospital as soon as possible, unless she's decided to have her baby at home. Most women choose to stay in the maternity ward of a hospital for the period of time before, during, and after the baby is born, where there are medical specialists, such as doctors and midwives. These places also have all the medical equipment needed, and drugs are available to help women who are in pain. If anything goes wrong, a hospital has more resources to deal with the problem, so it's usually the safest place to be.

Find the right word(s) in the text above for each of the clues below:

1. This means 'before birth'

2. The opposite of 'the most dangerous' (2 words)

3. The things that are needed for a particular activity or purpose

4. Patients can get medical advice and help here but they usually need an appointment (2 words)

5. Experience and be badly affected by an illness, disease or pain

6. Taking care of (2 words)

7. The process of being born

8. This adjective means 'expecting a baby'

9. Another word for 'illness'

10. These people are given special training to help women give birth

11. This means 'causes them to'... (2 words)

12. Throw up, or be physically sick

13. Everything that a person, an organisation or a country has, or can use, to do something

14. A large room in a hospital that women stay in before they give birth (2 words)

15. A verb used to say a baby 'comes out of its mother's body' (2 words)

/ 15

57. Children

It's amazing how quickly children develop when they're very young. In the first six months of life, babies cry, laugh and make other sounds. They move their eyes, and raise their legs and their heads. After a year, they sit and crawl, and may be able to stand, and after two years, they know how to walk, and then to run. When they're about four, they learn to walk up and down stairs, and a year later they can dance.

At the same time, children's minds are also developing. When they're two years old, they're capable of saying a few words, and before long they know about fifty words and their own name. At three, they ask questions that begin with 'what, where' and 'who', and can draw a person with a head. Adults understand children who are four years old, and their vocabulary is normally about 1500 words by this age. Their drawings are now of people with heads, legs and arms, and soon they're able to draw a house. When they're five, they learn to count using their fingers, and they know more about themselves, including their age and their birthday. They've already learnt how to speak, and it's about this age that they learn how to write a few letters of the alphabet, and copy squares and triangles.

Children go through several stages of development, from the time they're born to the time they become teenagers. At each stage they develop quickly, but the changes that take place in the early years, before they go to school, are amazing!

Find the right word(s) in the text above for each of the clues below:

1. Adults do this on chairs or sofas, but small children may do it on the floor

2. Lift or move something up

3. All the letters from A to Z

4. Move our bodies in time with the music

5. The day someone is born, or the day, every year, someone was born

6. When children do this, they're upset and tears come out of their eyes

7. Shapes with three straight sides

8. Children and young people who are older than twelve and younger than twenty

9. We have four of these and a thumb on each hand

10. Move around on hands and knees

11. All the words that someone knows, or are part of a language

12. A verb used to say someone's body is in a vertical position with their feet on the floor or the ground

13. We normally do this when we hear or see something very funny or amusing

14. Make pictures of something with a pencil or a pen

15. A noun used to say that someone or something becomes more advanced, stronger or larger

/ 15

58. Growing Up

Being a teenager isn't easy. Young people have to deal with all sorts of experiences. Their bodies grow quickly and change shape. They experience strong feelings and thoughts, which make them behave differently from before. They begin to understand more about who they are, being an individual and having an identity. They want to be liked by other children at school, and worry that they may not be. As they grow older, they learn more about love and sex as well, and who they are attracted to. Many argue with their parents. This stage of development is difficult for most young people and can be unhappy and painful. The good news is that it only lasts a few years.

As they get older, teenagers rely less on their parents and start to become more independent. Teenagers in the UK have to go to school, so they spend most of their time with people their own age. They learn the same things and share similar views of the world. They choose their own vocabulary and words to describe the world they are in. There are so many new decisions to make. Their parents used to make most of these decisions for them, but not any longer. They decide who they like, and try to make friends. They decide what to eat and drink, what to do in their free time, and what games or sports to play. They choose what clothes to wear, what music to listen to, and who to chat to on the phone or Internet. What they decide to do makes them who they are.

Find the right word(s) in the text above for each of the clues below:

1. Did something in the past but not now (2 words)

2. The form of something, for example, someone's body

3. What people have when they're not working or studying (2 words)

4. Choices made after thinking about what to do

5. Emotions

6. Mothers and fathers

7. Young people aged between 13 and 19

8. Continues for a particular period of time

9. All the words that someone knows, or are part of a language

10. Interested in someone in an emotional or sexual way (2 words)

11. Opinions, attitudes or beliefs

12. This means the same as 'depend'

13. Who someone is or what something is

14. Disagree with and speak angrily to someone

15. Keep thinking about problems or unpleasant things that might happen

/ 15

59. Adults

Adults have a lot of decisions to make. They decide what to do when they leave school. Some choose to work, others go to college or university. What job should they do, and where should they do it? Do they drive, cycle, walk, or take public transport? They make decisions about relationships, who they spend time with, and who their friends are. Do they stay single, live with someone, or get married? They decide whether to have children, or adopt children, and how many to have. Over the years and the decades, couples choose to stay together, split up or get divorced.

Would they prefer to be in a city, a town, or the countryside? Adults decide where to live, and whether they should rent or buy a flat or a house, with or without a garden. Do they have pets, and if so, what kind, and how many? They choose their furniture, and how their home should look. What food do they eat and what do they drink? Do they recycle, or throw things away? They decide where to go shopping, what to buy, what clothes and shoes to wear, what hairstyle to have. Where should they travel to, or go on holiday, and what do they do when they get there? They make decisions about the sports they play and their pastimes.

Adults choose how to spend their money or where to save it. They follow a religion, a political party, or a sports team. What type of music or radio programme should they listen to? Do they decide to spend time reading, and if so, what do they read? What TV channels, films, or plays should they watch? They choose the social media they're interested in, and who and when to call, email or text. It can't be easy being an adult in the modern world. They must be very grown up to make so many decisions!

Find the right word(s) in the text above for each of the clues below:

1.   Periods of ten years

2.   How someone's hair is cut or arranged

3.   Hobbies, or activities we do in our free time

4.   Buses and trains that people pay to use (2 words)

5.   Put money in a bank account and keep it there

6. Use money to pay for something, or take time to do something

7. Tables and chairs

8. Do something with paper, glass, clothes, or anything else so it can be used again

9. These are normally in a theatre, but can also be on TV or the radio

10. Become the legal parent of someone else's child

11. Have clothes, shoes, hats, scarves, gloves, glasses, contact lenses, make-up or jewellery on our bodies

12. Facebook, LinkedIn, and Twitter (2 words)

13. Another way of saying someone is, or behaves like, an adult (2 words)

14. Put things in the bin instead of recycling them (3 words)

15. Dogs, cats and other animals that live at home with us

/ 15

60. Education

In England, some children go to nursery school when they're very young, and most children go to primary school by the time they're six years old. When they're eleven or twelve, they leave primary school and go to secondary school, where they usually study a number of subjects. They take exams in these subjects in their mid-teens, usually at the age of sixteen, and the qualifications they get if they pass are called GCSEs, which is short for General Certificate in Secondary Education. The subjects they do usually include English, maths, and science, (biology, chemistry and physics), as well as history, geography, and design and technology.

After GCSEs it's possible for people to leave school and try to find work. Those who want to continue their education can apply to go to a college to study a particular subject. The subject they choose may be related to a type of work, so it could eventually help them get a job. The other option is to stay at the same school, or move to a different school, and do a two-year course called A levels, (short for Advanced levels). Students who decide to do A levels normally study between two and four subjects, and the subjects they choose are often the ones they did well in when they took their GCSEs. If they get good enough grades in their A levels, they may be offered a place on a course at one of the country's universities. After three or four years of study, assessment and exams, students graduate from university, which means they gain a degree in their subject. All the hard work they've done at school, at college, or at university, and the qualifications they've gained, could be a great help to them, not only when they start work, but in their future careers as well.

Find the right word(s) in the text above for each of the clues below:

1. The study of events that happened in the past

2. Written tests that students do at the end of an academic course

3. The language or literature of England as a subject

4. Students who get good A level results can do a degree course at one of these places

5. The study of numbers, shapes, and calculations with numbers

6. The qualification students get when they graduate

7. A subject that could be useful if you want to work in a pharmacy

8. The school that children go to before secondary school (2 words)

9. This word has a similar meaning to 'choice'

10. Children learn about computers in this subject (3 words)

11. A word which has a similar meaning to 'evaluation'

12. The study of the earth, places, products and populations

13. The study of plants and animals

14. A school for children between the ages of 2 and 5 (2 words)

15. The study of forces such as heat, light and sound, and the relationships between them

/ 15

WORK

61. Finding Work

Young adults are faced with challenges and responsibilities that can be very stressful and difficult. When they leave school or university, they need to decide what to do with their lives. Most people choose to look for a job and spend a period of time trying to find the right one. To be successful they need to convince an employer they have more to offer than the other candidates. Good qualifications achieved in education are important, but an employer often requires experience as well. In an increasingly competitive market, it's very difficult to find the dream job. It's often better and more realistic to apply for a temporary position or a job that isn't as well paid. By doing this there's a better chance of getting the opportunity to work and gaining the experience needed. People in temporary jobs can show their employer they work hard, get things done, and are an important part of a team. Whether they stay with the same company and get a promotion, or find a better paid or more senior position elsewhere, the initial period of employment will have been very helpful.

Find the right word(s) in the text above for each of the clues below:

1. This word can mean 'difficult' but here it means 'with a lot of effort'

2. First

3. New or difficult tasks that test people's abilities or skills

4. Knowledge and skills gained by doing something for a period of time

5. For a limited period of time. The opposite of 'permanent'

6. All the people applying for a job

7. A move to a better paid, more important or more senior job

8. A person or company that pays people to work for them

9. You get these if you pass your exams or successfully finish a course

10. All the learning and teaching at schools and universities

11. An adjective used for the achievement of something intended

12. A noun used for a time in a particular situation when something can be done

13. An adjective used for a situation in which people are trying to do better than other people

14. An adjective used for anything which causes a lot of anxiety, worry or mental pressure

15. Not pessimistic or optimistic

/ 15

62. Employment

If you want to find a job, you may need to complete an application form or a CV. A CV gives information about your personal details, education, training and previous employment. When you send this information to an employer, which can be done either directly or via an employment website, the employer will assess your qualifications and experience, and decide whether you should be shortlisted for the position. If you are shortlisted, you will be invited to attend an interview where you will be asked questions by a manager or a human resources officer, who is usually responsible for recruitment. If you do well at the interview you may be offered the job. Some companies offer training courses to new employees, and apart from receiving a salary, you will also get annual leave and may be able to join a pension plan. This means you will be given a pension many years later when you retire.

Find the right word(s) in the text above for each of the clues below:

1. A regular payment of money people receive at the end of their working lives

2. Selected for an interview from all the candidates

3. All the learning and teaching at schools and universities

4. Money that employees receive for doing their jobs

5. The number of days holiday an employee gets every year (2 words)

6. These would normally include your name, email address and mobile number (2 words)

7. People who work for a company or an organisation

8. Stop working

9. This is a formal word for a job

10. Finding, interviewing and employing someone

11. You get these if you pass your exams or finish a course successfully

12. A person or company that pays people to work for them

13. This means to think about and judge how good something is

14. Knowledge and skills gained by doing something for a period of time

15. The process of learning the skills needed to do a job

/ 15

63. Interviews

Getting the job you want can be difficult. A lot of unemployed people are looking for work. To be successful you have to do better than other people who apply for the position. An employer wants to know that you have the right skills, experience and motivation to do a professional job. You need to convince them you have what's required. Think about what you should write in your application.

What can you do to have the best chance? First of all, read about the company online so you learn more about it, and what it does. Make sure you know and understand all the words and expressions that you need to talk about the job. If you're invited to go for an interview, there should be an opportunity to impress the interviewer with your knowledge of the work you would do, and the company you've applied to join. It's also very important to let the interviewer know about any experience you've had that could help you do the job. Think carefully about the personal qualities you've got that could be useful, and what motivates you to do well. What else can you tell them that will encourage them to offer you the position? What questions will you ask at the end?

Your appearance is important too. Spend time deciding what to wear, so it's right for the job, the company and the occasion. Your hair, clothes and shoes should be clean. Start your journey early so you're not in a hurry, and are calm and ready when you arrive at reception. Employers don't like people to be late for work, so they won't be happy if you're late for your appointment! Finally, during the interview, listen carefully, be relaxed, be confident, and answer the questions in a positive and enthusiastic way.

Find the right word(s) in the text above for each of the clues below:

1. What you do when you complete an application form and send it

2. The reasons that make someone want to do something

3. A formal arrangement to meet someone at a specific time, often connected with work

4. How you feel if you really believe in yourself and your ability

5. An adjective used for people who haven't got jobs

6. We wear these on our feet

7. The opposite of negative

8. Make someone believe something

9. A noun, which is quite a formal word, used to say how someone looks

10. A meeting at which a person is asked questions and considered for employment

11. The opposite of 'dirty'

12. Phrases, or a couple of words, used to say something

13. This is sent to an employer when someone applies for a job

14. How you are if you feel and show that you're interested in and excited about something

15. An adjective used to say a job is being done well, or the right way, by someone qualified to do it

/ 15

64. People at Work

Some people are self-employed, but the majority of workers are employed by companies or organisations. Jobs in these companies can be either temporary or permanent, but nowadays it's very unusual for a job to be for life. Positions are full time, which would normally be more than 35 hours a week, or part time, if the work can be done in fewer hours or days of the week. Most people have their own jobs, but they also work as part of a team with other people, who are their colleagues. They report to a manager, who in larger companies is accountable to a more senior manager, who might be a managing director. Companies usually have at least one person whose job is in sales, another in marketing, and someone in a financial position, often a qualified accountant. Other employees deal with human resources, or HR, public relations, or PR, and information technology, or IT, and there's normally a customer services person or team to help resolve any problems. By employing people with different skills, knowledge and experience, companies are usually well placed to deal with most work issues and everyday tasks.

Find the right word(s) in the text above for each of the clues below:

1. This type of job could be 7 hours a day from Monday to Friday (2 words)

2. This department helps employees use computers and other electronic equipment (2 words)

3. This department helps to employ, train, develop and advise employees (2 words)

4. This department helps customers who need information or are unhappy about something (2 words)

5. This department gives official information about the company to employees and the public (2 words)

6. This department sells the company's products

7. This department gives information to people about the company's products and advertises them

8. Working for yourself (2 words)

9. A very senior manager in a company (2 words)

10. The people you work with

11. A type of job which is normally two or three days a week, or three or four hours a day (2 words)

12. The opposite of 'temporary'

13. A person who is qualified and works in a finance department

14. The opposite of 'minority'

15. Organisations that make money by producing or selling products

/ 15

65. Jobs

I recently asked the students in one of my classes what jobs they wanted to do when they left London and returned to their countries to find work. Many of our students are working as au pairs, cleaners, waiters and baristas, but these are temporary jobs while they're in the UK. What they would really like to do as a career, and the jobs some of them are doing now, are very different. These are some of the occupations they mentioned they were interested in, in no particular order: interior designer, engineer, IT specialist, accountant, farmer, estate agent, chef, architect, receptionist, journalist, and dentist. These are all jobs that people can hope to get and be successful in, provided they have the right qualifications, skills, and experience.

Find the right word(s) in the text above for each of the clues below:

Someone who...

1.   ... decides how the rooms in a house should look and be decorated (2 words)

2.   .... works as a cook in a restaurant and could be in charge of other cooks

3.   ... takes care of people's teeth

4.   ... designs buildings

5.   ... keeps animals and grows crops on land in the countryside

6.   ... writes news stories for newspapers or magazines

7.   ... designs and builds machines, roads or bridges

8.   ... helps you find a flat or a house to buy or rent (2 words)

9. .... deals with people's financial records

10. All the jobs, or the type of work, that someone does in life

11. Two capital letters used for people or departments responsible for computers

12. An adjective used for jobs that aren't permanent

13. These people live with families and look after their children (2 words)

14. If you go to a company or a hotel, you normally meet and speak to this person first

15. Particular abilities needed to do a job

/ 15

LEISURE

66. The Arts

Art, literature, music and theatre are often called the Arts, especially when we talk about them as a group. Art is a subject which can be studied at school, college or university. We go to art galleries or museums to see the visual arts: paintings, drawings, and ceramics by famous artists, and photographs taken by well-known photographers. Some forms of visual art are located outdoors and have become tourist attractions. Beautiful buildings designed by architects, statues, and other sculptures, can be viewed in the parks and squares of our cities and towns.

Literature refers to any written work which is considered to be artistic or intellectual because it's different from the ordinary language in everyday use. It comprises works of fiction; the novels, plays, poems and short stories created in the imagination of the writer. It also includes works of non-fiction; books about real people, events, and established fact, like biographies.

The theatre is where plays are performed, which is why theatre is often known as a performing art. Cinema, opera, ballet, dance and music concerts are also called performing arts, because in all of these, the artists or performers perform in front of an audience. Music is featured in almost all the performances. Classical music is a very important part of opera, ballet and some concerts, and it's used in plays and films as well. There are many other types of music, though, which are played in public performances, but are also enjoyed by people at home. When we listen to music, when we sing, dance, or play a musical instrument, we experience an art form which, in one form or another, is available to everyone.

Find the right word(s) in the text above for each of the clues below:

1. A story performed by a group of dancers with music but no talking or singing

2. Places we visit to look at artistic, historical or scientific objects

3. Long stories which become books and are about people and events created by writers

4. These pictures are created using brushes and oils or water colours

5. Bach, Beethoven and Mozart all wrote this type of music

6. Stories of people's lives which are written by other people

7. Pieces of writing, arranged on separate lines, which often rhyme

8. A group of people who watch and listen to a performance

9. Pictures which are created with a pencil, and not with paint

10. Novels are much longer than these pieces of writing (2 words)

11. Solid figures or objects made from wood, stone or metal

12. The art of making objects with clay, such as vases, jugs, bowls and pots, and the objects themselves

13. This means 'describes' or 'is connected to' something (2 words)

14. Hamlet, Macbeth and Romeo and Juliet are all examples of these

15. This is quite like a play, but it is performed by people who sing while music is played

/ 15

67. Entertainment

Entertainment is about providing or showing something interesting or amusing to people. It's for people to enjoy, and in the modern world it's also about making money. Many of us in the UK still go to the cinema, to sports events, music concerts, nightclubs and comedy clubs, but most forms of entertainment are now experienced at home.

Some of the most popular forms of entertainment are watching films or TV programmes, listening to music and reading books. Technology has changed the way we experience and enjoy entertainment. Information on the Internet and computer games are two examples of this, but almost any form of entertainment is now available online. Just as there are numerous types of music, there are also many different types of film, known as genres. These include action films, horror films, romantic films, comedies and thrillers. Most of these films are based on stories that were originally written and published as novels, biographies, or other works of fiction and non-fiction, so there are as many types of book as there are film genres. There are films on TV every day, and episodes of drama and comedy series are shown weekly. There's also a large variety of other programmes. Some of the most popular are soap operas, talent shows, and quiz shows, and for people who want to know what's been happening in the real world, there are documentaries and current affairs programmes. In the UK in the 1960s there were only three TV channels: BBC1, BBC2 and ITV. Nowadays there are hundreds of channels, so many in fact, that when we switch on the TV, we often can't decide what to watch!

Find the right word(s) in the text above for each of the clues below:

1. A word that describes films or books that are about love and relationships

2. Recent political or news events are in this type of programme (2 words)

3. Stories on TV about the lives and problems of a group of people played by actors (2 words)

4. TV programmes or films which give the facts or information about a real event or problem in the world

5. Films or TV programmes that are intended to be funny or amusing

6. Films with frightening characters, like Dracula (2 words)

7. A lot of fast and exciting things happen in these films (2 words)

8. This means the same as 'turn on' (2 words)

9. Films which have exciting and shocking stories, often about crime

10. A story which is on TV every week for a number of weeks

11. An adjective used for anything that you can get, buy or find

12. In these programmes people try to answer questions (2 words)

13. Scientific knowledge used to create and improve machines

14. An interesting or exciting story which is often a play made for TV

15. We use the remote control for the TV to choose one of these

/ 15

68. Music

There are many different types of music, some of which originated much longer ago than others. People have enjoyed listening to classical music and jazz for centuries, and country music has existed since the 1920s. Pop, reggae, soul, and R&B, have all been popular for at least fifty years, as have rock and disco. In recent decades, hip hop, rap, dance, and techno, amongst others, have also become popular.

Most musicians who perform these types of music are either solo artists, or in groups and bands. Some of them are vocalists, and others play a large variety of instruments, such as the guitar, the drums, and keyboards. Classical musicians, who play instruments like the violin and the piano, may decide to join an orchestra. Jazz musicians, whose instruments include the saxophone, the trumpet, and the double bass, often play as members of a jazz band.

Some people learn to play a musical instrument and others have singing lessons. Those lucky enough to have good voices can sing on their own, or with other people, (in a group of singers, or a choir). A few of the best and most talented musicians, who play their musical instruments or sing in front of audiences, eventually become famous and wealthy. Successful musicians tended to have a recording contract and go to a studio to record their songs, and these were played on the radio and on TV. Times have changed, though. Nowadays music can be downloaded and much of it is listened to on a desktop or laptop computer.

Most people only play musical instruments as a pastime. They play music on their own, or for their family and friends, usually because it's fun and they enjoy it.

Find the right word(s) in the text above for each of the clues below:

1. A musical instrument with strings that you hold under your chin

2. A room where music is recorded

3. Another word for 'rich'

4. A large musical instrument with a keyboard of black and white keys

5. Another word for 'singers'

6. You hit this round instrument with two sticks, or with your hands

7. People who sing together in a church or other public place

8. Musicians who perform on their own (2 words)

9. An adjective used for people who have a lot of natural ability

10. This is a wind instrument that a musician blows into. It's larger than a trumpet

11. Moved from a large computer system to a smaller one

12. A group of people who play classical music together with different musical instruments

13. A written agreement between a musician and a music company (2 words)

14. These are used by people to sing, and some are better than others!

15. A musical instrument with strings. Some are acoustic, others are electric

/ 15

69. Hobbies

A hobby is an activity that people do to relax or for pleasure in their free time. When adults aren't working, and children aren't at school, a lot of us spend time on our hobbies. Most hobbies used to take place at home but computers and technology have made it possible for many of these activities to be done anywhere, indoors or outdoors. We watch TV and films and listen to music on public transport. We use social media and play games in coffee shops and parks. Traditional games like Monopoly, Scrabble and chess were once played on boards, and crosswords and puzzles were in newspapers and books. Nowadays they can all be played or done on screens. People used to do creative writing with pens and paper, but most of it now is done using a keyboard. There are creative hobbies, though, that haven't changed that much, such as painting, drawing, cooking and playing musical instruments. Some of us enjoy making things, too, like clothes, jewellery and models, and collecting coins and stamps.

A number of pastimes usually take place outdoors because being outdoors is an important or necessary part of the activity. Gardening and metal detecting, for example, as well as camping, fishing and flying kites, are all outdoor activities. Walking, sailing, and golf are all sports, but they're hobbies too, and are normally outdoor activities for the same reasons. Most other sports, though, can be played either outside, or inside at a leisure or sports centre.

Find the right word(s) in the text above for each of the clues below:

1. A word which means the same as 'free time'

2. Rings, necklaces, bracelets and earrings

3. Another way of saying 'in your own flat or house' (2 words)

4. If you want to do this activity you need a tent

5. People who do this hobby hope to find something valuable or interesting in the ground (2 words)

6. If you like making meals in the kitchen, this is one of your hobbies

7. A game that's played with kings, queens, bishops and castles

8. These could be made of wood or plastic and are stuck together with glue

9. This is another word for 'inside' (a building)

10. Another word for 'hobbies'

11. A hobby for people who enjoy growing flowers and plants

12. These objects are attached to a long string and move around in the air

13. These are used as money and are made of metal

14. Houses and hotels can be bought in this game

15. People stick these on envelopes before they send letters or cards in the post

/ 15

70. Sports and Places

Tennis and badminton are played on a court with a net in the middle. In tennis you hit a ball over the net, but in badminton you hit a shuttlecock over the net, (which is higher than a tennis net). Squash is also played on a court which looks like a large, empty room, and you hit a ball against the front wall. So is basketball, but the aim is to throw or drop a ball into a basket at the end that you're attacking and the other team is defending. It's not easy to do this, though, because the top of the basket is ten feet, or just over three metres, above the ground. Football, rugby and cricket are all played on large areas of short grass which are called pitches. In football and rugby, the pitches are rectangular, but in cricket they're circular. In football there are goals with nets at both ends, and in rugby there are posts at both ends in the shape of the letter 'H'. If you go to watch these sports played by professionals, the venue would normally be a stadium with a pitch inside the stadium.

There are different venues, though, for other sports. Horse racing takes place at a racecourse and golf is played on a golf course. We can watch athletics at an athletics track, motor racing at a race track, and cycling at a cycling track or in a building called a velodrome. We swim and play water polo in swimming pools, some with diving boards at one end, and there are pools in many sports and leisure centres. Whatever we want to do, there's usually somewhere we can do it!

Find the right word(s) in the text above for each of the clues below:

1. Tennis, squash, badminton and basketball are all played on this

2. This sport is played with a ball in a swimming pool (2 words)

3. The opposite of 'back'

4. Drivers in fast cars compete against each other in this sport (2 words)

5. You run on this in the 100 or 200 metres (2 words)

6. Football matches are played on these surfaces

7. This is green and mowed short so matches can be played on it

8. The opposite of 'full'

9. These are above swimming pools (2 words)

10. A large building that professional football matches are played in

11. In this sport you have to pass the ball backwards, but you can kick it forwards

12. These people are paid to play a sport. They aren't amateurs

13. Jockeys hope to win by riding as well as they can at this venue

14. Places where sports events, concerts and conferences are held

15. This is the opposite of 'lower'

/ 15

THINGS

71. Sports Equipment

If you want to play a sport you need to have the right equipment. For tennis, table tennis or squash, you need a racket / racquet and some balls, and if you play badminton you need a racket / racquet and a shuttlecock. For a sport like football or rugby, you'll have to find a pair of boots that are the right size and a ball that's the right shape; a football is round and a rugby ball is more of an oval shape. You wear a swimsuit, or swimming trunks, and goggles for swimming, and for cycling you'll need to buy a helmet and a bicycle, which is expensive. The equipment you need for golf can also be expensive because you have to buy about ten clubs, a bag to put them in, and plenty of golf balls. It's easy to lose balls on a golf course. If you want to play snooker, billiards or pool, you'll need a cue and the right balls for each sport. All three sports are played on a table with pockets in the corners and on the sides.

A sport which is very popular in the UK, but you may never have played in your own country, is cricket. To play cricket you need a cricket ball, a cricket bat to hit it, or 'bat' with, as well as a helmet and a pair of pads that you wear on your legs for protection. There are eleven players in a team, and one of the players, called a wicket keeper, stands behind a piece of equipment called a wicket, which is made of wood. The wicket keeper needs two pairs of gloves to play cricket. One pair to bat with, and a much larger pair to keep wicket with!

Find the right word(s) in the text above for each of the clues below:

1. A woman or a girl would wear this in the pool.

2. Badminton players try to hit this over the net

3. This is what you hit the balls with if you play pool

4. All the things that you need to play a particular sport

5. The opposite of 'cheap'

142

6. Another name for this sport is 'ping-pong' (2 words)

7. There are fifteen red balls in this sport. The other balls are yellow, green, brown, blue, pink, black and white.

8. A type of hat that protects your head if you're on a bike, or a motorbike, or you're playing cricket.

9. You wear these on your feet when you play football or rugby

10. If you're a golfer you hit the ball with these

11. The balls are placed on this before you start a game of snooker

12. These protect your eyes and help you see underwater

13. The shape of an egg and a rugby ball

14. Words that often go before 'glasses, lenses, socks, shoes, boots, shorts' and 'trousers' (2 words)

15. The long word for 'bike'

/ 15

72. Tools

A tool is an object that you hold in your hand and use to repair, make things, or do something else with. Hammers and screwdrivers are two of the most useful tools. In many homes they're kept in a container called a toolbox. Hammers are normally used to put nails into pieces of wood. To do this, a nail has to be hit quite hard with the flat end of the head of a hammer. At the other end of the head there's a claw, which is used to remove nails from wood.

A screwdriver is usually used to put a screw into a piece of wood, metal or plastic, and a good example of an object that we use it with is a plug, attached to the end of an electrical appliance. Another tool, which is also an electrical appliance, called a drill, is used to make holes in a wall or some other surface. Once this has been done, a screw can be put into the hole and tightened with the drill, which can also extract screws whenever this is required. Most of us have a hammer and at least one screwdriver at home, but drills are normally used by builders, carpenters, and people who do DIY, (do it yourself)!

Metal detectors aren't used to fix or make anything, but they are tools, and they have a number of different uses, some of them extraordinary. They're used during and after wars to find landmines, and at airports and other places to check people's bags. They're also used in buildings to locate metal pipes and other objects hidden above ceilings, below floors or behind walls. Metal detecting has become a popular pastime too. People enjoy looking for objects made of metal wherever they think they might be, including fields, beaches, gardens and parks. Most metal objects in the ground, like bottle tops and nails, aren't of any real interest. When something old, unusual, or valuable is discovered, though, it can be very exciting for the person who finds it. Metal detectors can detect objects made of gold, silver and bronze, jewellery such as rings and earrings, and some interesting coins, many of which are hundreds of years old!

Find the right word(s) in the text above for each of the clues below:

1. A tool with a long handle and a heavy metal head

2. People whose job is to make and repair wooden objects

3. This has to be put into a power point if you want to use an electrical appliance

4. Another word with a similar meaning to extract, or take out

5. Another word with a similar meaning to fix or mend

6. A tool which is used to tighten or loosen screws

7. An electrical appliance that makes holes

8. The outside or top of something, which is often flat

9. Use a screwdriver to put one of these into a piece of wood

10. Use a drill to make this in a wall

11. Use a hammer to hit this into a wall or a piece of wood

12. You can keep all your tools in this

13. The opposite of 'loosened'

14. Hobby

15. A machine, such as a hairdryer or a vacuum cleaner, that we plug into a power point (2 words)

/ 15

73. Work and School

I work in an office. I keep a lot of useful things in my office that I use every day and which help me do my job. I've got a desk with drawers which contain a wide variety of stationery. Nowadays diaries and calendars are available online, but I like to have manual ones in my office as well. I keep my diary in the top drawer of my desk, together with highlighters, paper clips, scissors, a ruler, a stapler, and a notebook. There's plenty of room in the bottom drawer of my desk for some of the larger items, such as packets of A4 paper, and envelopes of different sizes. I've got a briefcase too, which I bring to work with me in the morning and take home in the evening. Everything else I need to do my job I tend to have in my briefcase, including a pencil case. I keep a sharpener, an eraser and a correction pen in the case, as well pens and pencils, so wherever I am, I've always got something to write with. My children have many of these things at school and use some of them during their classes, but their stationery's much more colourful than mine!

My laptop, printer, phone and a calendar are all on my desk. On one side of the desk there's a cupboard that has all my files in it, and on the other side I keep a small bin to put rubbish in, and a larger one for paper, cardboard, and anything else that can be recycled. Outside my office there's a corridor which leads to other offices and a meeting room. The meeting room, which is at the end of the corridor, has a large, round table in it, a whiteboard on the wall, a flip chart in one corner, and a coffee machine in another. When we have meetings, we usually start with a cup of coffee, before we talk about the work we're doing, and try to make decisions!

Find the right word(s) in the text above for each of the clues below:

1. These are used to cut pieces of paper, plastic or cloth

2. This is used to remove pencil marks from paper

3. Small pieces of metal that hold several sheets of paper together (2 words)

4. A small computer that can be moved and carried easily and quickly

5. This contains tiny pieces of metal which fix pieces of paper together

6. Teachers write on this with special pens during a class

7. This contains a white liquid that covers written mistakes. It's often called Tippex. (2 words)

8. These contain information on a particular subject and can be kept in a cupboard or on a computer

9. An object that cuts the end of a pencil so the pencil isn't blunt

10. Special pens which mark words in a text in bright colours

11. Pens, pencils, paper and envelopes are all examples of this

12. This helps you draw straight lines on a piece of paper

13. A small book with lined paper or blank pages in it that you can write information on

14. A machine that reproduces words and pictures on pieces of paper

15. If you want to throw something away, put it in this

/ 15

74. Bathroom Things

There are lots of things in the bathroom to help me get ready every morning. Most them are above, below, or next to the basin. The hot and cold taps are just above the basin, which we fill with water whenever we want to wash our face or hands.

I keep a tube of toothpaste, my toothbrush, a flannel and some soap beside the basin. There's also a razor and some shaving foam that I use to shave, and a mirror above the basin so I can see what I'm doing! It's on the front of the bathroom cabinet, which is on the wall, and has a lot of useful things in it. Inside the bathroom cabinet on the top shelf I keep a small pair of scissors, a few plasters in case I cut myself and a tube of antiseptic cream to stop the cut becoming infected. On the bottom shelf there's a bottle of aftershave, for me, and a bottle of scent, which is sometimes called perfume, that my wife uses. I keep other things on the bottom shelf as well, including a deodorant, which I use under my arms, a hairbrush so I can brush my hair, and a comb if I want to comb it. Below the basin there's a cupboard where we keep toilet rolls, bottles of shampoo, and shower gel. We keep packets of soap and toothpaste there as well, in case we run out of anything. This is also where I put my washbag which I put everything in whenever we go away.

Find the right word(s) in the text above for each of the clues below:

1. This helps prevent infection (2 words)

2. I keep my toothbrush, toothpaste, flannel, razor and a can of shaving foam in this when I'm away.

3. I use this to clean my teeth. It's electric

4. I put these pieces of material on cuts to protect my skin

5. Finish or use up (3 words)

6. A piece of furniture like a small cupboard which we keep things in (2 words)

7. This is often called a face cloth

8. A substance which we put under our arms to stop body smells

9. I look in this every morning when I shave

10. This is what some men put on their faces when they shave (2 words)

11. I use this to remove the hairs from my face when I shave

12. A liquid in a plastic container that's used for washing the body (2 words)

13. A liquid with a pleasant smell that men put on their skin

14. These are used for cutting fingernails

15. This is sold either as a liquid or a bar

/ 15

75. Kitchen Things

When we get back from the supermarket, we carry everything into the kitchen and start taking food out of our shopping bags. Any frozen food goes into the freezer, and we put all our fresh food, such as vegetables, fruit, and dairy products, in the fridge. Tinned food, cans of drinks and anything else that won't go off are stored in the larder, which is normally cool, but not cold like the fridge.

The meals we have every day are prepared in the kitchen. We use the large oven in the cooker to roast or bake food, the microwave oven to heat it or for ready meals, and the hob when food needs to be steamed, boiled or fried. Once we've finished eating, we sometimes do the washing up in the sink with a dishcloth and dry everything with a tea towel. Most of the time, though, we use the dishwasher. When we take crockery out of the dishwasher, it's all put away in two cupboards, or on long shelves between the cupboards. We keep our mugs and cups in one of the cupboards, and glasses for water, wine, and soft drinks in the other. Plates, bowls, and saucers are arranged on one of the shelves.

Below the shelves there's a worktop, (the surface we prepare food on), and just below the worktop, there's a drawer containing all our kitchen utensils and cutlery. Under the drawer there's a large cupboard which has our saucepans, a frying pan and a baking tray in it.

Whatever it is, there's a place for it in our kitchen!

Find the right word(s) in the text above for each of the clues below:

1. A large cupboard or a very small room which is used for keeping food cool

2. It's used for cleaning crockery and cutlery in the sink

3. We eat soups and cereals out of these deep, round dishes

4. This has four hotplates and is used to cook anything in a saucepan or a frying pan.

5. A phrasal verb which means that food is no longer fresh (2 words)

6. Milk, yoghurt, butter and cheese (2 words)

7. Heated to 100 degrees Celsius

8. Spoons, knives and forks

9. Plates, bowls, mugs and cups

10. If you want to cook something in the oven you can put it on this (2 words)

11. Food prepared before it was bought that only needs to be heated (2 words)

12. Kept (in a place) for future use

13. You can drink tea or coffee out of a cup, or one of these

14. A large cloth used to dry the washing up (2 words)

15. Sieves, spatulas, ladles and potato mashers! (2 words)

/ 15

76. Finding Accommodation

When someone arrives in a city or town for the first time they need to find accommodation, which is somewhere to stay or to live. They may be able to stay with friends or find a room in a house and become a lodger. If they don't know anyone, they should contact an estate agent, who can help them find a property to rent, which would usually be a flat or a house. If it's a flat, it's important to know whether it's a basement flat, a ground floor flat, or a first, second or third floor flat. Of course, if it's in a large block of flats it could be much higher up. There would probably be a lift in the building and there may be a panoramic view, (a view of a wide area of land), from one or more of the windows. Estate agents normally have the keys for all their properties so they can give people a guided tour and show them what the flat or house looks like inside.

The owners of properties are called landlords or landladies. They let properties to tenants, who are the people who rent them. This is why you see signs outside flats and houses which say 'to let'. Estate agents also help people buy flats and houses, but property is expensive, so most people need to go to a bank and get a mortgage. Banks normally only agree to give people mortgages if they have jobs and earn enough money to be able to afford the repayments.

Find the right word(s) in the text above for each of the clues below:

1. This person helps people buy or rent houses and flats (2 words)

2. The opposite of 'lower down' (2 words)

3. Men who own properties and let them to tenants

4. The money a bank lends someone to help them buy a property

5. A flat which is on the same level as the street outside (3 words)

6. A general word for a place to stay, live or work in

7. A general word for a building, and any land that is sold or let with it

8. A flat which is below street level (2 words)

9. A person who rents a bedroom and lives in the house

10. Landlords or landladies do this to a property if they want a tenant to move in and pay rent

11. A word that means someone has enough money to pay for something

12. This takes someone up to a higher floor or down to a lower one

13. A tall building which has apartments in it (3 words)

14. These have information on them in the form of words, pictures, or both

15. People who rent properties

/ 15

77. Houses
....

There are different types of house in the UK. In the cities and towns many are terraced houses, but in rural areas a large number of houses are detached or semi-detached. Houses in the countryside often have gardens, but in urban areas, where there's less space, a house may only have a small back garden or no garden. Houses usually have two or three floors, but there may be a basement below, or an attic above these floors. When you go through the front door, in many of them there's a room called a hall, or a corridor, which leads to the other rooms. On the ground floor most houses have a sitting room and a kitchen. There may be a separate utility room, dining room and possibly a downstairs bathroom or toilet. If anyone living in the house works from home there could also be an office. In most houses the bedrooms and bathrooms are upstairs on the first or second floors and there's a flight of stairs that you go up to reach them. Some elderly people who find walking difficult live in bungalows, which don't have any stairs.

Find the right word(s) in the text above for each of the clues below:

1. A room or a building where people work and sit at desks

2. This adjective is the opposite of 'rural', and means 'town' or 'city'

3. You walk up this if you want to get to the floor above (3 words)

4. This describes a house which is not attached to any other house

5. People sit at a table and have meals in this room (2 words)

6. These houses have a ground floor but no other floors

7. A row of houses which are attached to each other

8. Another word for 'loft'

9. An adjective that describes people and means the same as 'old'

10. If the washing machine isn't in the kitchen it might be in this room (2 words)

11. An adjective that means 'countryside'

12. This type of house is joined to another house on one side only

13. Get to

14. You go through the front door into this area or room

15. A long, narrow area in a house or building with rooms next to it

/ 15

78. Furniture

When we moved into our house, we put some furniture in every room. In the kitchen and the dining room there are tables and enough chairs for our family and friends. In the sitting room, we've got a large sofa, a comfortable armchair, and several chairs for people to sit on. The lamp next to the sofa gives us enough light to read, and when we're sitting down we like to put hot and cold drinks on our coffee table. There's also a television, a bookcase and a large cupboard in the room, and a framed painting on the wall. In our bedroom, there's a double bed, with a bedside table on either side, a wardrobe, a chest of drawers and a dressing table. The children all have single beds and chests of drawers in their rooms, and we've recently put a sofa bed in the spare room.

Most of our furniture is modern, but a few years ago we went to an antique shop and bought some furniture which is more than a hundred years old. The side table and the stool we chose are by the front door in the hall. We put the antique desk we bought in the office, and the grandfather clock on the landing at the top of the stairs. I don't often visit antique shops, but when I do, I go inside and see whether there's anything for sale that's beautiful or interesting. If I think there is, and I can afford it, I like to buy it and take it home.

Find the right word(s) in the text above for each of the clues below:

1. You can sit on it during the day, or sleep in it at night (2 words)

2. A place which sells old and valuable objects such as furniture or jewellery (2 words)

3. This is wide enough for several people to sit on. It has cushions, and it's comfortable

4. This is only wide enough for one person to sit on, but it's more comfortable than most chairs.

5. Clothes which aren't put on hangers are folded up and kept in this (3 words)

6. This piece of furniture has shelves with books on them

7. I sit and work at this in my office

8. The ones in the kitchen have been built in, but this one in the sitting room hasn't.

9. It still tells the time, even though it's very old (2 words)

10. A wooden seat which has legs, but no arms or back

11. A tall piece of bedroom furniture used for hanging or storing clothes in

12. This has drawers and a mirror, and you sit in front of it (2 words)

13. This has a shade and a stand and helps us see better

14. Of the present, or recent times, and not of the distant past

15. Another word for a picture created by an artist

/ 15

79. Gardens

A garden is an area of land which is next to a house, and could be at the back or front of the house, or both. Some large gardens extend to the sides of houses as well and most people have hedges, fences or walls which separate their gardens from those of their neighbours.

Part of the garden usually has grass growing in it, and in some gardens vegetables and fruit are also grown. The area of grass which is cut short is called a lawn, and in other parts of the garden the grass is often allowed to grow, so it's longer and there could be a lot of weeds. Most people grow plants and flowers in their gardens which can be put in the earth or soil, or in pots. Some people also have a greenhouse, where their plants are protected from bad weather, and others have sheds where gardening equipment can be kept or stored. A gardener might keep a pair of gardening gloves, a spade and a fork in the shed, as well as a lawnmower, a wheelbarrow, and perhaps even a hosepipe. Finally, a patio in the back garden is a good place to put a table and chairs. Having a drink or a meal there on a sunny day can be a very enjoyable experience, but in the UK the weather isn't always warm enough for us to sit outside!

Find the right word(s) in the text above for each of the clues below:

1.   This building has glass sides and a glass roof and is used for growing plants in

2.   Wild plants which grow in gardens and are usually removed by gardeners

3.   A part of the garden with grass which has been mowed

4.   The people whose houses or flats are next door or nearby

5.   Gardeners wear these on their hands to protect them (2 words)

6.   This means that something is put and kept somewhere so it can be used later

7.   Leaves, soil or gardening equipment can be carried in this. It has a wheel and two long handles.

8. A gardening tool with a flat metal surface which is used for digging in the garden

9. A gardening tool with three or four sharp metal points which is also used for digging

10. The top part of the earth in the garden where vegetables or flowers grow

11. A small wooden or metal building where gardening equipment and tools are stored

12. A hard flat area behind a house where people can sit and eat outside

13. These are usually made of wood or metal and form the boundary between two fields or gardens

14. Attach this to a tap at one end, and water the garden with it at the other!

15. Rows of small trees or large bushes that are planted along the edges of gardens or fields

/ 15

80. An Evening In

In the winter, when it's cold and dark, I look forward to going home after work and enjoying an evening in. When I arrive home I switch on the lights, close the curtains and change into more comfortable clothes. I tend not to wear a sweater because we've got central heating. There are radiators in the sitting room and in our bedrooms, so most of the time it's warm and cosy. This probably explains why our gas and electricity bills are higher than they should be!

When my flatmates get home we decide what we're going to do and quite often we choose what we're going to watch on TV. We sometimes watch a film; an action movie or a comedy, but we also like documentaries, news and sports programmes. At the end of the news we watch the weather forecast so we know what the weather's going to be like the next day. We normally cook something at home, but at the weekend we sometimes order a home delivery pizza or an Indian curry. We could get a take away or go out to eat because there's a restaurant near where we live, but in winter, once we get home, we usually prefer to stay in.

Find the right word(s) in the text above for each of the clues below:

1. The opposite of 'lower'

2. Large pieces of cloth that cover a window and are opened or closed

3. A service provided by a restaurant which brings food to your flat or house (2 words)

4. A system which sends hot water round a building through pipes (2 words)

5. TV or radio programmes which give the facts or the true story about something

6. A dish made with meat or vegetables and spices, which is often served with rice

7. A TV programme that tells us whether we can expect sunshine or rain (2 words)

8. This item of clothing is also called a jumper or a pullover

9. These tell you how much you have to pay for your food, water, gas or electricity

10. This programme is about international, national or regional events that happened today and yesterday

11. A film or programme intended to be funny or amusing

12. The opposite of 'light'

13. You go to a restaurant to collect this and return home with it (2 words)

14. This means 'warm and comfortable'

15. The hot water from pipes goes into these metal objects and heats a room

/ 15

81. Cities

Cities are important towns which tend to have much larger populations than other parts of a country. Thousands, and in many cases, millions of people live and work in these places, so they can be crowded and noisy. In fact, in excess of 50% of people in the world live in cities, and this number could increase to more than 75% in the next few decades. Many of the largest of these, including capital cities, now have skyscrapers, train stations, underground railways and airports.

Most people who live in cities take public transport or drive to work, but some choose to cycle or walk. During the rush hour there's usually a lot of traffic on the roads and there are commuters on the trains and buses. The majority of these commuters live in the suburbs or on the outskirts of the city, but visitors and tourists often stay in the city centre. There are shopping centres and department stores for those who like to go shopping, and anyone who wants to take exercise can go to a sports or leisure centre, or to one of the parks. Larger cities, like London, have numerous museums and art galleries that are open during the day, and theatres and cinemas that you can go to in the evening as well. There are plenty of restaurants and bars to choose from, serving food and drink from early in the morning until late at night, and if you decide to stay up late, you could go to one of the clubs and experience the nightlife. It doesn't matter which city you visit or happen to live in, there's always something to do!

Find the right word(s) in the text above for each of the clues below:

1. A general word for entertainment that people can enjoy in a city in the evening

2. Transport systems known as the Subway in New York and the Tube in London (2 words)

3. Very big shops which sell a large variety of products (2 words)

4. People go to these places to see objects which are historical, scientific, cultural, or artistic

5. These areas of a town or city are furthest from the centre

6. The largest or most important cities, or where governments are located (2 words)

7. People who travel to and from work every day

8. Very tall buildings in cities

9. The period of time when most people travel to work or return home (2 words)

10. If you want to fly to another city or country you need to go to one of these

11. Areas of public land in cities where people can walk, play or relax

12. There are some famous paintings and sculptures in these places (2 words)

13. How a street or a market full of people could be described

14. Plays and musicals are performed in these places

15. The areas between the city centre and the outskirts of a city

/ 15

82. The Countryside

The countryside, or the country as it's sometimes called, is really anywhere outside urban areas, such as cities and towns. The houses and cottages in the countryside that people live in are normally in villages, on farms, or located some distance from other buildings. Some countryside is very flat, but in other areas there are hills, and even mountains, and valleys. Much of the land is covered either in woods and forests, where wild animals live, or fields, where farm animals are kept and farmers grow crops. It's a great place to go for a long walk, enjoy the fresh air and see some wonderful views and scenery. Most of it is inland, but it extends to the coast as well, next to the sea. There are also areas of water that are right in the middle of the countryside, such as lakes and ponds, and streams that descend from the mountains and become rivers. Life in the countryside is usually quieter, more peaceful and more relaxed than in the cities, which makes it a good place to retire for older people who no longer work.

Find the right word(s) in the text above for each of the clues below:

1. Areas of land between and below hills or mountains

2. These are like small lakes in the countryside or people's gardens

3. Areas of land with buildings where crops are grown and animals are kept

4. You can normally walk up these. They're smaller than mountains

5. An adjective used for animals or plants which grow and live in their natural environment

6. Small houses which are usually in the countryside

7. A comparative adjective which is the opposite of 'noisier'

8. Plants which are grown in large quantities on farms

9. People live in these places, but they're smaller than towns.

10. An uncountable noun which is used for all the views we enjoy in the country

11. These are much narrower, shorter and smaller than rivers

12. Farmers keep cows and sheep or grow crops in these places. They usually have a fence around them

13. These are like small forests

14. An adjective used for land which is all on the same level, with no hills, valleys or slopes

15. It's a pleasure to breathe this when we're in the countryside (2 words)

/ 15

83. Giving Directions

We went for a long walk in the countryside on Sunday. We had a map, but after an hour or so we arrived at a village and weren't sure where to go. We decided to ask for directions. Luckily we saw a woman who lived in the village and said she could help. This is what she told us:

"The footpath you're looking for is on the other side of the village. Turn left here and follow the road until you arrive at a country lane, just after the village shop. Keep walking down the lane, which bends to the right, until you see a pub and a few houses on your left. Go past all the buildings, and take the first left over the bridge. After about a hundred metres the road forks. You need the road that goes off to the right. Follow it up the hill. When you get to the farmhouse at the top, walk along the path between the house and the field on your right. You'll see a sign pointing to your left which is where you'll find the footpath. It should take you about ten minutes to get there. Good luck!"

Find the right word(s) in the text above for each of the clues below:

1. A verb that's used to say how much time is needed to do something

2. A place people go to meet that sells alcoholic and soft drinks, and usually serves meals.

3. People in the village buy their groceries from this place

4. 'Continue' (doing something)

5. This may tell you where to go, but unlike a map, you can't take it with you

6. A verb used for a road that changes direction to the left or the right and is no longer straight

7. A verb used for a road that divides and becomes two roads, one to the left and the other to the right

8. Walk or drive over this to cross the river or the road below

9. Information about how to get to a particular place or location

10. Change direction to the left or the right, or around!

11. People walk along this but it's too narrow for cars

12. A word with a similar meaning to 'beyond' and 'after'

13. Another way of saying 'arrive at' using different words (2 words)

14. A drawing or a plan which shows where all the places are in a part of the countryside, a city or a country

15. Showing or indicating the direction or the way to a particular place with an arrow (or a finger)

/ 15

84. The Seaside

We went to the seaside in July. The weather forecast said it would be hot for several days, so we packed our bags, put on our sunglasses, and headed for the coast. The beach we went to, which has always been my favourite, is sandy, and it's never very crowded. When we arrived at ten in the morning it was already hot enough to sunbathe. We sat on the large beach towels we'd brought with us and put on some suncream, and hats to protect us from the sun.

When there's good weather and the skies are blue, the view out to sea is spectacular. Beautiful yachts and other boats of various shapes, sizes and colours move slowly across the bay. There's an island on the horizon, and you can see and hear the seagulls flying above the waves. The sea near the beach is shallow. It's a lovely temperature on a warm day in summer, refreshing but not cold, so people enjoy going in to swim, and playing games in the water. On the beach there's a café that serves sandwiches, ice creams and cold drinks, and a hut nearby where the lifeguards work. They watch what everyone's doing to make sure we're all safe and no-one's in any danger in the water. Next to the sandy area in front of the hut, and to the left, are some rocks and a number of rockpools. Children go there with nets and buckets to catch shrimps, (which are like small prawns), and tiny crabs.

Find the right word(s) in the text above for each of the clues below:

1. The opposite of 'deep'

2. Large white birds with grey feathers that live near the sea

3. Creatures that can walk sideways

4. Where the sky appears to meet the land or the sea

5. What we can see from a particular place or position

6. These are used to catch fish and seafood

7. Land which is completely surrounded by the sea

8. We dry ourselves with these, and we lie on them when we're on the beach

9. People who work on a beach or next to a swimming pool

10. These are worn to protect our eyes and help us see better

11. Sailing boats

12. Spend time on a hot day trying to get a tan

13. An area of the sea which is partly surrounded by land

14. All the land in a country which is next to the sea or the ocean

15. We put this on our skin to stop it burning when the weather's hot

/ 15

85. Places to Visit in London

When tourists visit London or students come to the city to learn English, there are lots of interesting places to see. There are parks such as Richmond Park where people go to walk, cycle or to see the deer that live there. Other animals can be seen at London Zoo and for people interested in trees and plants Kew Gardens is a good place to go to. There are historic buildings such as the Houses of Parliament, the Tower of London, St Paul's Cathedral and Buckingham Palace. If you like art, and in particular, paintings, go to Trafalgar Square where you'll find the National Gallery, or the National Portrait Gallery, which is nearby. There's so much to see in the museums that a visit to the British Museum or the Science Museum would be a great idea. There are also some unusual buildings to see from the outside such as the London Eye, the Shard and the Elizabeth Tower. You can visit all of these places by taking the Tube, but going on a boat cruise on the River Thames, or an open top bus tour through the streets of the city, would be more fun!

Find the right word(s) in the text above for each of the clues below:

1. This was a prison for hundreds of years and the Crown Jewels are kept here (4 words)

2. Beautiful animals that can be seen in some of our parks

3. This tourist attraction is a huge wheel by the river that goes round and round (3 words)

4. Enjoyable or amusing

5. A well-known art gallery that's just round the corner from the National Portrait Gallery (3 words)

6. If you're learning physics, chemistry or biology, this is a good place to visit (3 words)

7. Lions, elephants and giraffes are kept here (2 words)

8. Portraits and landscapes are two examples of these

9. If you're interested in botany, this is a good place to visit (2 words)

10. The funerals of Nelson and Churchill took place here, and Princess Diana was married here (3 words)

11. Big Ben is the bell of a clock at the top of this building (3 words)

12. The British Royal Family live here (2 words)

13. A journey for people to enjoy and see the sights by sea or on a river

14. This place is almost three times the size of Central Park in New York (2 words)

15. A journey around a building, a town, a city or a country

/ 15

TRAVEL

86. Planes and Flying

Planes, (the long word is aeroplanes), are very large vehicles with wings and several engines. They're extremely heavy, but their engines are powerful enough to lift them off the ground. A plane starts every journey on a runway, which is like a road next to an airport. From a stationary position it starts to move forward, before it accelerates and travels along the runway at great speed. Then, in no time at all, it leaves the ground, goes up in the air, and into the sky. When this happens we say the plane is taking off.

Before take off, the captain welcomes all the passengers, (the people travelling on the plane), and tells them about the flight and the weather. When the plane is ready to fly, there's a safety demonstration, and the crew check that everyone has put on their seatbelts, (which have to be worn on a plane for safety reasons). A few minutes after the plane has gone up in the air, the passengers normally undo their seatbelts. They can relax and have something to eat and drink. They may also listen to music, watch a film, play games or read. Business people can do some work if they want to.

The passengers put on their seatbelts again when the journey is almost over. The plane then flies down towards the land. When this happens we say the plane is landing. Once it's on the ground again, it moves slowly along the runway until it gets to the airport. Soon after it stops, the captain thanks everyone for choosing to fly with the airline and wishes them a pleasant stay in the city or country they've just arrived in. The passengers then undo their seatbelts, take their hand luggage, get off the plane and walk into the airport.

Find the right word(s) in the text above for each of the clues below:

1. All the people who work on a plane (or a ship)

2. An adjective which means 'not moving'

3. Starts to go faster

4. An adjective that tells us something weighs a lot

172

5. This shows passengers what to do in an emergency (2 words)

6. When a plane leaves the ground and moves into the air, it's doing this (2 words)

7. When a plane leaves the air and returns to the ground, it's doing this

8. The parts of planes, cars and ships that produce the power they need to move

9. If something has great power or force we use this adjective to describe it

10. Leave the plane (2 words)

11. Suitcases and bags

12. A journey by air in a plane or helicopter

13. Planes have these and so do birds!

14. Open something so it is no longer attached

15. This means 'in the direction of' something

/ 15

87. Airports

If you're going take a flight, (a journey by air), to a city in another country, you'll need a ticket, which you can buy online, and your passport. The day you fly you should try to get to the airport early with all the information that's required, including your flight details. Make sure you pack everything you're going to need when you get to your destination, and know exactly what you have in your bags. At airports you have to go through customs on both departure and arrival. Everything that leaves and is brought into the country is checked.

Once you've arrived at the airport and found the right terminal, check the screens which give you information about your flight. They tell you if your flight is on time or delayed. They also tell you which gate to go to when it's time to board your plane. It's a good idea to check in as soon as you arrive. When you check in, you show your ticket and give your bags to the person who's working for the airline you're flying with. You're allowed to take hand luggage with you and put it in the lockers above your seat, but not larger cases and bags. These are placed in the hold. As soon as you've checked in you can go to the departure lounge. Have a good flight!

Find the right word(s) in the text above for each of the clues below:

1.   A formal word for 'leaving an airport'

2.   A formal word for 'arriving at an airport'

3.   Flat surfaces on TVs and computers that show information or pictures

4.   All the bags that are small enough to take on the plane with you (2 words)

5.   Large, heavy cases and bags are put in this part of the plane

6.   A formal word which means 'get on' a plane

7.   This means the same as 'permitted'

8. A very large vehicle with wings and powerful engines

9. An official document that identifies you as a citizen of a particular country

10. This means something happens when it should happen (2 words)

11. This means something happens later than it should happen

12. A barrier that can be opened and closed, or the way out of an airport

13. A building at an airport where people start or end their journeys

14. Your bags are checked here when you leave and arrive at an airport

15. A company that flies people to different places on their planes

/ 15

88. Boats

Boats are vehicles that travel on water, and there are many different types of boat. Large boats are called ships, and some of these ships carry passengers across oceans and seas. Boats that travel shorter distances, known as ferries, transport people along rivers, or from one country or island to another nearby. Ferries, for example, travel across the Channel between England and France, a journey that usually takes less than a day, and between England and Spain, normally an overnight crossing. There are cruise ships which go round the world, stopping at different ports so people can see and visit interesting places during the cruise. On voyages which take days or weeks, passengers have cabins so they can sleep at night, and they sit on seats or at tables during the day. Most of these ships have shops, bars and restaurants, and on some there are cinemas, casinos and swimming pools! The floors or levels on ships are called decks and the round windows are known as portholes.

Some of the largest and heaviest ships are cargo ships, which take goods to other countries to be bought and sold. Many of these transport products in vast containers, and food is kept in refrigerated containers to keep it fresh.

Other boats are much smaller than ships. We rely on fishing boats to catch the fish and seafood we eat, and lifeboats rescue people who are in trouble at sea. Boats are used for sport and for leisure too. There are rowing boats on our rivers, yachts on our lakes and at sea, and people on holiday hire boats to travel along our canals.

Find the right word(s) in the text above for each of the clues below:

1. Sailing boats

2. The Pacific and the Atlantic

3. Long journeys by sea

4. Ships that people have holidays on (2 words)

5. Part of the Atlantic Ocean between Dover and Calais (2 words)

6. Small rooms on ships which are for sleeping in

7. Boats used in emergencies to save people's lives

8. Boats used when universities race against each other on the River Thames (2 words)

9. Products transported by sea, air, rail or road so people can buy and sell them

10. Look out of one of these to get a view of the ocean

11. Man-made waterways

12. Prawns and crabs

13. Large areas of water, smaller than seas and surrounded by land

14. Ships that don't normally carry passengers (2 words)

15. Towns or cities where ships arrive and leave

/ 15

89. Holidays

People go on holiday throughout the year, but summer holidays are more popular than holidays in the winter. During the summer months they travel to places where they can enjoy warm weather and sunshine. The weather in the UK can be warm and sunny, but it can also be cold, cloudy and wet, so people go abroad to countries like France, Spain, Italy and Greece. They stay in hotels, apartments, and campsites and spend much of the day at the seaside. They sunbathe on the beach, go swimming in the sea, or might choose one of the sports or activities available. Sailing, surfing, diving, hiring boats, water-skiing, and walking along the coast are all popular activities.

Some people prefer skiing holidays to beach holidays. Skiing holidays are in the winter months, and one of the most popular places to ski in Europe is the Alps. These are mountains that cover a huge area in eight different countries, including Austria, Switzerland, Germany, France and Italy. People who go skiing also hope to have good weather, and good snow for skiing is important. Skiers take warm clothes with them on holiday because it can be very cold on the slopes. When they arrive at their ski resort they normally hire everything else they need, including skis, sticks, boots, helmets and goggles.

Find the right word(s) in the text above for each of the clues below:

1. The sides of mountains or hills in skiing resorts

2. An area on the coast where people go for beach holidays

3. Protective headgear

4. You'll be sleeping in a tent if you go to one of these places

5. A sport in which someone's pulled across the sea, or a lake, by a motorboat

6. A journey or a holiday on a yacht

7. A mountain range (2 words)

8. Skiers and swimmers wear these over their eyes

9. Do this if you want to get a tan

10. Where people stay and also where they ski (2 words)

11. Hold these in your hands when you ski

12. Wear these on your feet and attach them to your skis

13. Swimming underwater

14. White, soft, and essential for skiing

15. Trying to stand on a board and riding the waves

/ 15

90. Sightseeing and Tourism

If you don't want to go on holiday to lie on a beach or ski down a mountain, you could travel to a country you've never been to before. There are so many things to see and experience when you become a tourist. You can stay in an old city and go sightseeing, or travel across a country and enjoy its beautiful scenery. If you choose to do some sightseeing, a good place to start is the nearest tourist office. The brochures there are normally available free of charge. You may have to pay for a guidebook, but it will tell you where everything is and you won't get lost. See the sights you've read or been told are worth seeing. You can visit historic places like cathedrals and castles, or walk around an art gallery. If it's a sunny day and you'd rather be outside, why not go to one of the busy markets? Buy some souvenirs to take home to your family and friends. Take photos of the buildings and the squares, the statues and the fountains. Walk through one of the parks or go on a tour of the city.

In the evening you can stay in your apartment or your hotel if you're tired, or go out and enjoy the nightlife if you're not. Try some of the local food. In big cities, there's a choice of hundreds of restaurants, bars and nightclubs. See a show or a film. Go to a concert or a play. Whatever you do, have a great time!

Find the right word(s) in the text above for each of the clues below:

1. Visiting and looking at interesting buildings and places

2. A performance with actors on stage in a theatre

3. You don't have to pay for something if it's this (3 words)

4. Very similar to churches, but larger

5. If you know where to go, this won't happen to you (2 words)

6. A building in which there are paintings on most of the walls (2 words)

7. Water features in the squares of cities and towns

8. Bought on holiday and taken home to remind people of the holiday

9. Information and advice is available here (2 words)

10. A person who visits a city or a country for pleasure, not business

11. Built for people to live in, and to stop their enemies getting in

12. Indoor and outdoor places where food, clothes and other goods are sold

13. Like guidebooks, but with less information and fewer pages

14. Objects made of stone or metal, many of which are of people or animals

15. A performance with singing and dancing

/ 15

91. Learning to Drive

Driving a car is a skill that people need if they want to get a driving licence and drive safely on the roads. The best way to learn is to have driving lessons with a qualified driving instructor. They sit beside you in the passenger's seat and explain what you have to do. You can choose to learn in a car with manual gears, which are operated and controlled by hand, or if you prefer you can learn in an automatic car. Automatic cars have a number of gears, including P for park, R for reverse, N for neutral and D for drive. Learner drivers, however, are advised to learn in a car with manual gears. This is because, in the UK, if you pass your test in a manual car you can also drive an automatic car. If, however, you learn to drive in an automatic car you won't be allowed to drive a car with manual gears.

There are many other things you need to learn as well, and one of the most important is the expression "mirror, signal, manoeuvre". Before you drive around a roundabout, or turn left or right into another road you should always look in your mirrors first. Then you indicate, or signal, with your indicator so other drivers and pedestrians know what you're about to do. Finally you manoeuvre, which means you change your speed, your direction or your position. If this sounds difficult, don't worry! Your driving instructor will teach everything you need to know, and you'll be able to practise it again and again until you drive well enough, and safely enough, to pass your test.

Find the right word(s) in the text above for each of the clues below:

1. Anyone sitting next to the driver is sitting in this (2 words)

2. Permitted

3. A small light that lets other drivers know you're going to turn left or right

4. Another word for 'indicate'

5. Manually (2 words)

6. What trainee driving instructors become when they pass their exams

7. You have to pass your driving test and get one of these before you can drive on your own

8. A word used for the gear that moves a car backwards

9. The opposite of 'dangerously'

10. A person whose job is to teach people a practical skill like driving, or a sport

11. Do an activity regularly, so you get better at it

12. The opposite of 'fail'

13. A circular part of a road which vehicles go round to join another road

14. Drivers look in these to see what's happening behind them

15. Change direction to join another road on the left or the right

/ 15

92. Gears and Pedals

Gears are controls that make cars move. If you want to drive in a car with manual gears, one of the important things to learn is how to change gear. When you start the engine, the car is in neutral gear which means the engine isn't moving the wheels. You move from neutral to first gear to move the wheels forwards, but if you want to go backwards, you move from neutral to reverse gear.

When the car's moving forwards, and as it goes faster, you move up the gears from first, to second, then third, fourth, fifth, and in some cars, sixth gear. Fifth and sixth gear are normally used when a car is being driven at higher speeds on main roads and motorways. When you want to slow down you move down from fifth (or sixth) to a lower gear. Change gear from the lower gear to neutral again just before you stop or park.

There are three pedals which you operate with your feet. The one on the left is called the clutch. When you press your foot on the clutch you can change gear. This is difficult at first but drivers who practise it enough will find it gets easier. The pedal in the middle is the brake. This helps you slow down and stop. To stop the car properly you also need to put on the handbrake, especially if you've parked on a slope. The pedal on the right is the accelerator which is used to increase or reduce speed. There are many other things you need to learn about driving, but once you know how to use the pedals and change gear, everything else should be easier!

Find the right word(s) in the text above for each of the clues below:

1. The power needed to move a car forwards or backwards comes from this

2. The gear between third and fifth

3. Stop your car and leave it for a period of time before coming back to it

4. A word that means push something with, for example, your finger, hand or foot

5. The gear used to move a car backwards

6. The opposite of 'slower'

7. The pedal used to make the car go more quickly or slowly

8. The pedal used to change gear

9. The pedal used to slow down and stop the car

10. This makes sure your car doesn't move at all, especially if you're parked on a slope

11. Circular, rubber objects which are the only parts of a vehicle on the ground

12. Push down on this with your foot to make something move or work

13. The opposite of 'increase'

14. A surface, such as a hill, which isn't flat or horizontal

15. Make something work

/ 15

93. Public Transport

In cities like London, millions of people travel from one place to another every day. Without public transport there would be far too many cars on the roads. There would be traffic jams everywhere.

Public transport for many people is the quickest, cheapest and most convenient way of travelling in a city. The underground railway in London opened in 1863. It's known as the Tube and has trains on different lines which cross the city in every direction. Three of the busiest and most famous are the Northern line, the District line and the Central line. The stations and many of the lines are actually above the ground. Escalators, lifts and stairs move people from one level to another so they can catch a train to work or to go home.

Buses also cross the city in every direction. In London many of them are red and have two levels, a lower deck and an upper one, where people can enjoy views of the city. They take longer to reach their destination because of the traffic, but are a good way to travel unless you're in a hurry. There are cars, and bikes, that people can hire too, and there's even public transport on the river, so they can travel by boat.

Find the right word(s) in the text above for each of the clues below:

1. A superlative adjective used to say there's more happening than anywhere else or any other time (2 words)

2. A lot of vehicles which are either stationary or moving very slowly on the roads (2 words)

3. A vehicle that travels on water

4. Stairs which move and carry people from one level to another

5. One of the levels or floors on a bus or a ship

6. Pay to have or use something for a period of time

7. People cycle on these

8. The opposite of 'below'

9. These machines have doors that open and close. They carry people from one level to another in a building

10. Where we should arrive at the end of any journey

11. This means you're doing something quickly because you're short of time (3 words)

12. You go to one of these places if you want to catch a train

13. A long name for the Tube (2 words)

14. Useful, easy, or quick, and with no problems

15. Trains travel on these from one station to another

/ 15

94. Coaches and Trains

People who want to travel from one city or town to another may choose to drive. Long journeys, however, can be exhausting and not everyone has a car or can afford to pay for the petrol. For people without much money, travelling by coach is a good option. It's normally cheaper than driving or going by train, and coaches travel to most towns and cities, where many of them end up at a coach station. Victoria Coach Station in London is a well-known destination. Coaches arrive here from, and travel to, a large number of other places in the UK, and some parts of Europe.

Coaches are usually more comfortable than buses. They're also faster than buses, partly because buses tend to travel within cities and towns, rather than between them.

Trains can be a relaxing and enjoyable form of transport, and it's often quicker to go by train than by any other form of transport, apart from a plane or a helicopter! Trains travel across the country from the north to the south and the west to the east. They're made up of a number of carriages which are also called coaches. Most of the carriages are for passengers to sit in, but there's usually at least one buffet carriage where food and drinks can be bought, and on some there are small restaurants as well. One disadvantage, though, is that it can be very expensive to travel by train. Going by road on a coach or sharing a car with friends normally costs much less.

Find the right word(s) in the text above for each of the clues below:

1.   Using something with other people, often at the same time

2.   The place someone or something is going to, or has been sent to

3.   A type of aircraft powered by a revolving, horizontal rotor

4.   This means having enough money to buy or pay for something

5.   A noun used to say something is less useful or worse for a particular reason

6.   If you're in England, this is where Scotland is

7. If you're in Wales, this is where Ireland is

8. This is where coaches start and finish their journeys (2 words)

9. Another name for train coaches

10. Very tiring

11. Another word for 'choice'

12. Nowadays, with electric cars, we depend less on this type of fuel

13. A room or counter selling light meals or snacks

14. Inside

15. A noun used for travelling long distances between cities or countries

/ 15

95. Safety on the Roads

Anyone thinking of riding a motorbike or cycling should realise how dangerous it can be. Cars, vans and lorries share the roads with motorbikes and bikes. Motorcyclists and cyclists are injured or killed every week when they are hit by larger vehicles and knocked off their bikes. Governments try to make people aware of the dangers and improve safety, but it's still a tragic situation. Wearing a helmet to protect their heads is essential, and anyone on a motorbike or a bike, or driving a car, should take extra care. They ought to check their mirrors to see whether any other vehicles are near them, and must do this before they turn left or right, or join another road.

The other people who need to be careful, especially when they cross the road, are pedestrians. Trying to cross a road where motorists don't expect it can be very dangerous. Pedestrians should use pedestrian crossings, and only cross the road when the traffic lights turn green.

If there's a serious accident anywhere in the UK, call 999 as soon as possible. The emergency services arrive at the scene as soon as they can get there. They're able to arrive at most accidents quite quickly, even when there's a lot of traffic on the roads. This is not only because their vehicles are driven at high speed, but also because of their sirens and flashing lights. When other people in cars hear a siren or see flashing lights in their mirrors, they try to move over to the side of the road so an ambulance, a police car or a fire engine can go past them. The emergency services save thousands of lives every year when they drive across our cities and towns to help people who have been in an accident.

Find the right word(s) in the text above for each of the clues below:

1. These tell motorists when they have to stop and when they can go (2 words)

2. Parts of the road where cars have to stop to let people walk across (2 words)

3. People who drive cars

4. A formal word for bikers, or people who ride motorbikes

5. People who ride bicycles

6. People who walk on pavements or across roads

7. This is worn to protect someone's head

8. This means the same as 'considering' (2 words)

9. An adjective that describes a bright light that goes on and off

10. Make something better

11. A place where something unpleasant happens, often an accident or a crime

12. Make sure someone is not hurt or injured or something is not damaged

13. An adjective that describes a situation when someone is killed or badly injured

14. People injured in an accident are taken to hospital in this

15. This makes a loud noise when an ambulance, a fire engine or a police car goes to the scene of an accident

/ 15

SAFETY AND SECURITY

96. Medical Emergencies

You should always get help as soon as possible in an emergency. In the UK you do this by calling 999 and speaking to the emergency services. You'll be able to tell them whether you need the fire service, the police, or an ambulance. If it's a serious medical problem, they'll send paramedics to you in an ambulance. Call 999 at once if someone has serious chest pain, and could be having a heart attack, or a stroke. Call them as well if a person is unconscious, has stopped breathing or is finding it difficult to breathe. Their lips might be going blue. If they've eaten or drunk something which you think is poisonous, call 999. If they've got a deep cut and are bleeding heavily, a bad eye injury, or a serious burn, call 999. If you're not sure what needs to be done, try to stay calm and ask the emergency services. They'll tell you what to do on the phone, and may explain how to put someone into the recovery position if they've lost consciousness but are still breathing. They can do this while you wait for the paramedics to arrive.

In less serious situations where it isn't an emergency but someone doesn't feel very well or has had a minor accident, ('minor' means less serious), call 111. You may be able to give the person first aid, especially if you've been on a first aid training course. Even if you haven't been trained, there are first aid kits and guides to basic first aid that could help you deal with the problem. You should be able to help with an insect bite or a sting. A bruise, a minor burn, or a cut can be treated as well, as can a minor sports injury, but if you think it's a broken bone, get medical help.

Find the right word(s) in the text above for each of the clues below:

1. Losing blood from the body

2. A vehicle used to take sick or injured people to hospital

3. A blue, brown or purple mark that appears on a person's skin

4. The emergency service that goes to the scene of a crime (2 words)

5. Ambulance workers who treat people injured in accidents

6. This happens when blood can't reach the brain because a tube (called an artery) is blocked, or there's bleeding in the brain

7. Immediately (2 words)

8. Here it's an adjective, but it's usually a noun which means becoming well again after illness or injury

9. Asleep, or not able to use the senses because of illness or injury

10. An injury caused by fire or heat

11. A wasp or a bee can hurt a person with this

12. A mosquito, an angry dog or a snake can hurt a person with this

13. Medical equipment kept in containers used to give simple medical treatment (3 words)

14. The external part of someone's mouth

15. An adjective used to say something will cause sickness or death if it's swallowed

/ 15

97. Safety at Home

To avoid injuries, keep rooms and stairs free of clutter, especially on the floor. If objects are left on the floor, people can easily trip and fall. Any water on the floor should be cleaned up at once, so people don't slip and hurt themselves. If a glass object breaks, use a dustpan and brush or a vacuum cleaner to remove any broken glass so people don't cut their hands. Glass left on the floor could result in serious injury; anyone with bare feet could cut themselves badly. If you're doing gardening or DIY, use the right equipment and wear the right clothing and shoes. Never do a job which you don't have the skills or experience to do safely. Be very careful with ladders, lawnmowers and gardening tools.

To prevent a fire, use a smoke alarm and test it regularly. Fires can spread quickly, so everyone must know how to get out of a building as soon as possible. All gas and electric heaters should be checked regularly, and replaced when they're old. Don't use flexes that are damaged or put too many plugs into one electrical socket; you could cause a fire. Keep clothes, furniture and curtains away from all heating appliances, such as cookers. Be very careful with candles, cigarettes, lighters and matches. An adult should always be in the room when they're lit and put out. Finally, never touch electrical appliances with wet hands or take one into the bathroom. Water conducts electricity, and being electrocuted could kill someone. Your home should be the safest place in the world. Make sure it is.

Find the right word(s) in the text above for each of the clues below:

1. Metal wires covered in plastic used to carry electricity to electrical appliances

2. Plastic objects (attached to flexes) which are put into power points

3. Appliances with a grill and an oven

4. Machines used for a particular purpose in homes

5. These are made of wax and are burnt to produce light

6. These are used to climb up walls or the sides of buildings

7. A noun used for a lot of untidy things in one place!

8. A verb used to say someone's foot hits something and they fall or almost fall

9. A verb used to say that someone's foot slides on the ground and they fall or almost fall

10. Machines used to cut the grass in people's gardens

11. Allows electricity or heat to move through something

12. A small plastic or metal container that dirt or glass can be brushed into

13. Not covered by any clothes or shoes

14. This makes a noise to warn people of smoke or a fire (2 words)

15. Move from one place to a larger area

/ 15

98. Looking after Children

Kitchens can be dangerous places for small children. If you're cooking, whenever possible, use the hotplates at the back of a hob, or the gas rings at the back of a stove. Place pan handles away from the front of the cooker so children can't reach them. Kettles should also be out of reach. Don't put hot drinks near the edge of a table, put them nearer the middle, so children can't knock them over. Keep sharp objects such as knives in drawers and always make sure children are a safe distance away when they're being used. Plastic bags should be kept away from babies and toddlers as well, because of the risk of suffocation. Cupboards which can only be reached by adults and can be locked would be a good place to keep them. It's important to be careful in the bathroom, too. Small children should not be left on their own when they're having a bath or near the hot water tap. Fill the bath with cold water, then carefully with hot water, and always check the temperature before a child gets into it.

Medicines and household or garden chemicals should be kept away from children to prevent babies or small children swallowing them or burning their skin. Gardening equipment like lawnmowers and sharp tools should also be stored out of children's reach, locked in a garden shed if you have one. Make sure children are a safe distance away from any equipment when it's being used. Whenever there's a barbecue, a bonfire, or fireworks, keep children well away. If you're walking on the pavement, however, or across or near a road, hold small children's hands and keep them as close to you as possible.

Find the right word(s) in the text above for each of the clues below:

1. Appliances used to boil water

2. Hit them by accident so they fall over (3 words)

3. Pedestrians in towns and cities walk mostly on this

4. Hold, pick up and put down a saucepan with one of these (2 words)

5. In the UK, people enjoy watching these light up the sky on the 5th of November

6. Kitchen or living room furniture with doors and shelves

7. Moving food or water from your mouth through your throat

8. This means the same as 'near'

9. An adjective used for anything that could easily cut someone

10. Dying because there is no air to breathe

11. A meal or a party outside where food is cooked over a fire in a metal container

12. The opposite of 'safe'

13. Most desks and cupboards have these

14. How hot or cold something is

15. Small children who have just learnt to walk

/ 15

99. Preventing Burglaries

A large number of burglaries are committed when burglars get into properties through unlocked doors or windows. It's best to make sure all your doors and windows have proper locks and are locked every time you go out. Front and back doors should be strong and at least four centimetres thick, and have a deadlock, a type of lock that needs a key to open or close it. A burglar alarm will also help prevent a break in. Ensure the sign for your alarm is in a visible place on the wall near the front door. This alone is likely to deter anyone thinking of breaking in. Put all your valuables in a safe place in your property, either locked away or somewhere they can't easily be found. Don't put them anywhere they can be seen through a window.

When you're out, it's a good idea to leave a light on in one of the rooms because it will make people think there's someone at home. If you're going away for a holiday or some other reason, don't tell anyone you don't know well, and never leave this information on an answering machine. Burglars often find out people's numbers and call them to see if they're at home. A fence can help prevent a burglar from getting into your back garden, but it needs to be high enough for him to have trouble climbing over it. Put locks on the doors of garden sheds and garages as well, because valuable objects worth hundreds of pounds, and cars worth thousands, are kept there. Being part of a neighbourhood watch scheme can also help, as can a dog. A burglar can't be sure whether a dog will bite him, but he won't normally take a chance!

Find the right word(s) in the text above for each of the clues below:

1. People keep their cars in these places

2. The local area that you and other people live in

3. If someone breaks into your home, this should go off and make a loud noise (2 words)

4. 'Have difficulty' (2 words)

5. An adjective used to say something is worth a lot of money

6. An adjective used to say something isn't easily damaged or broken

7. Houses and flats

8. These are used to close windows and doors so they can't be opened from the outside

9. People who break into properties to steal

10. Make someone decide not to do something because it wouldn't be good for them

11. The opposite of 'thin'

12. Going up something

13. This is made of metal or wood and it separates a field or a garden from land next to it

14. Can be seen

15. Stop someone doing something or something happening

/ 15

100. Pedestrians and Cyclists

Pedestrians should always find the safest place to walk and to cross a road. On busy or main roads they're advised to use subways or footbridges wherever possible. On pedestrian crossings it's important to wait until the lights turn green. If there's a traffic island in the middle, they should treat the two roads as two different crossings. Otherwise they could choose a place to cross where they can see clearly in all directions. They must make sure, though, that motorists, motorcyclists and cyclists can see them too. Before they cross, they should remember to look left, look right and then left again. Traffic can often be heard before it's seen, so it's a good idea for pedestrians to listen carefully as well.

Cyclists are much safer if they wear helmets and keep a safe distance between themselves and all other vehicles. It's dangerous for them to overtake on the inside of other vehicles. In the UK, some of the worst accidents happen when they try to overtake lorries or cars which are about to turn left, and don't see them. They should always use lights when it's dark or there's poor visibility, and wear brightly coloured clothing that helps drivers see them during the day. Finally, they must do what traffic lights and signs tell them to do. Going through a red light can cause a serious accident.

Find the right word(s) in the text above for each of the clues below:

1. People who drive cars

2. People who ride bicycles

3. People who walk on pavements and across roads

4. People who ride motorbikes and are sometimes called 'bikers'

5. The opposite of 'light'

6. All the vehicles that are on the roads at a particular time

7. When these are red you have to stop and when they're green you can go (2 words)

8. A place in the middle of the road where you wait until it's safe to cross (2 words)

9. Hard hats which protect people's heads if there's an accident

10. The opposite of 'the most dangerous' (2 words)

11. Unpleasant events that no-one expects and can cause injuries or damage

12. Places where it's safe to cross the road and there are often traffic lights or traffic islands (2 words)

13. Go past another vehicle

14. Large vehicles which carry goods

15. How far or well you can see, especially in good or bad weather

/ 15

ANIMALS

101. The Animal Family

I was amazed to discover that rabbits, squirrels, mice, and rats, are some of our closest relatives! Once I found out, I wondered whether other mammals were related to each other as well. When I looked at pictures of deer, camels, and giraffes it occurred to me that they might be close relatives. They're different sizes, but they all have long, thin necks and legs, and their faces are quite similar, so I wasn't surprised to find out that they were. I was, though, very surprised to discover cows and pigs happen to be related to whales and dolphins!

While we're on the subject of mammals, have you ever looked at a photo of a seal and been reminded of any other animals? Their bodies are different, but whenever I look at a seal's face I can't help thinking of dogs with similar faces, eyes and whiskers, and in particular, black labradors. They may have gone their separate ways 50 million years ago, but seals and dogs are related too.

Female mammals give birth to their babies and feed them with their milk, which makes them different from birds, and reptiles such as crocodiles, snakes and tortoises, all of which lay eggs. Mammals are also different from birds because, with one exception, they can't fly. Can you think of a mammal that has wings and can fly?

The answer to the question is bats, the only flying mammals on Earth!

Find the right word(s) in the text above for each of the clues below:

1. These animals have two humps and live in the desert

2. The largest of all mammals

3. The tallest animals in the world

4. The plural form for these animals is without an 's'. The males have horns on their heads shaped like branches

5. They look like alligators and live in rivers and lakes in hot countries

6. This means 'give food to'

7. Farm animals whose milk many of us drink

8. Animals with hard, round shells on their backs. They move very slowly

9. These animals have red, black, brown or grey fur, and long tails

10. What mothers do when they have babies (2 words)

11. These animals have long ears and live in holes in the ground. Some are kept as pets

12. A sea animal that lives near the coast and spends some of its time on land

13. Mammals that live in the sea, and are very intelligent and sociable

14. Long hairs that grow on animals' faces

15. A word which means the same as 'very surprised'

/ 15

102. How Animals Look

Animals are amazing creatures. No wonder there are so many wildlife programmes. It's fascinating to see how they behave in the wild and what they look like. Animals are all shapes and sizes, from the largest whale or elephant to the smallest mouse. Crocodiles, sharks and snakes look prehistoric and dangerous, which is probably because they are! Others that don't look dangerous at all can be very dangerous; chimpanzees and poisonous frogs, for example. Some animals have beautiful patterns on their bodies. Tigers and zebras, for instance, have stripes, and cheetahs and leopards have spots.

Many of the birds, reptiles, amphibians and fish on our planet are very colourful. Some are black and white but others are red, orange, yellow, green, blue or purple. These creatures are, in fact, all the colours of the rainbow. Two of the most colourful types of bird are parrots and flamingos / oes. There are also frogs, butterflies and lizards, which are all sorts of different colours. The chameleon, a type of lizard, can even change the colours on its own body!

Mammals like dogs and cats tend to be less colourful. Their fur can be black, white, brown, ginger or yellow, but few other colours. One exception, though, is the male mandrill, which is a large monkey. Charles Darwin believed it was the most colourful mammal in the world. It has dark green or grey fur and its bottom is bright pink and blue. It also has a long, red nose, a bright blue face, and a yellow or orange beard!

Find the right word(s) in the text above for each of the clues below:

1. How people, animals or objects appear to someone who sees them

2. We have hair, but many animals' bodies are covered in this

3. Crocodiles, snakes and lizards

4. Frogs and toads

5. Regular shapes or colours on carpets, curtains or animals' bodies!

6. A mixture of red and blue

7. A mixture of black and white

8. A mixture of light brown and orange

9. Hair that grows on a person's (or animal's) chin

10. From a time in history before information was written down

11. These reptiles look a bit like tiny crocodiles

12. Flamingoes are mostly this colour

13. How people or animals act or interact with each other

14. A curve of different colours in the sky when the sun shines through the rain

15. An adjective used to say a colour is strong and easy to see

/ 15

103. How Animals Move

Animals' bodies, and where they live, have a lot to do with how they move. Snakes slither along the ground because they haven't got any legs. Lizards and other reptiles crawl on four legs and so do frogs and toads. Insects crawl too, if they can't fly, or when they aren't flying. Most birds fly because they have wings, and bats fly as well, as do insects with wings, like wasps, bees and flies. Almost all animals move forwards, whether they're in the air or on land, but crabs have legs which are better at moving them sideways, so that's what they do!

Fish, dolphins and whales swim because they live in water and their bodies have evolved to move in water. Animals that live on land and in rivers or the sea can also swim, like crocodiles and penguins. Monkeys, squirrels and koala bears live in trees, so they know how to climb, (and some monkeys swing from tree to tree if they need to move fast). Mountain goats and tree frogs can climb too. Their names tell us where they go climbing! Frogs and toads hop and jump, and so do insects like grasshoppers, and mammals like kangaroos.

Most animals with four legs can run, and some, like cheetahs and lions, can run at great speed. Horses run very quickly as well, but we normally say they gallop rather than run. Of course, human beings only have two legs. We can run too, but there's a large bird with two legs that can run much faster than we can. It's called an ostrich!

Find the right word(s) in the text above for each of the clues below:

1. When horses do this, all four feet are off the ground in the middle of each movement

2. Use arms and / or legs to move through water

3. This is how some animals without legs move

4. When humans do this, they jump on one leg, but animals use more than one leg to do it

5. The opposite of 'backwards'

6. Going up a mountain, a hill or a tree

7. These animals are related to mice and rats. They have long furry tails

8. Animals move around on this surface (outside buildings)

9. Koala bears are native to Australia and so are these other animals

10. Human babies do this on their hands and knees. Animals normally use all their legs to do it

11. These insects are yellow and black. Like bees they can sting, but unlike bees, they don't make honey

12. Developed over a long period of time

13. Moving through the air

14. An adverb which has the same meaning as 'fast'

15. Move backwards, forwards or sideways, hanging from a branch

/ 15

104. How Animals Sound

There are words in the English language for many of the sounds that animals make. The ones we use the most are made by our pets, or animals that live near us or on farms. Dogs bark when they're excited and growl when they're being aggressive. Cats miaow / meow when they want something and purr when they're happy. Horses neigh and donkeys bray. Cows moo and sheep bleat and baa. Pigs grunt, ducks quack, cocks crow and hens cluck. Most pets and animals on farms make some sort of sound. Even mice do. If you listen very carefully when you see a mouse, you may hear it squeak.

Wild animals in Africa and other continents also make sounds. People who go on safaris hear these animals during the day, but some of the sounds they make at night are amazing. Birds sing, whistle, tweet or twitter. Monkeys chatter and lions roar. Elephants trumpet, wolves and wild dogs howl, frogs croak and snakes hiss. Even insects make sounds. Bees and flies buzz. In hot countries one of the loudest noises at night is the sound of crickets chirping and we often hear mosquitos / oes whine before they bite us!

Find the right word(s) in the text above for each of the clues below:

1. This sound is made by insects that make honey

2. This sound is made by insects rubbing their wings together

3. A cat which is enjoying something may make this noise

4. The verb used for a noise made by a tiny insect

5. The verb used for a noise made by a large animal. The noun is a musical instrument!

6. When small dogs do this again and again it can sound like a 'yap'

7. Some animals make this sound when they talk quickly and continuously

8. The sound that female chickens make

9. The sound that male chickens make early in the morning

10. The word for this sound rhymes with 'howl'

11. The word for this sound rhymes with 'car'

12. The word for this sound rhymes with 'speak'

13. The word for this sound rhymes with 'spoke'

14. The word for this sound rhymes with 'bray'

15. The word for this sound rhymes with 'back'

/ 15

105. World Records

The world is a much more interesting place because we share it with so many extraordinary animals. Animals, of course, are very different from us, but some of them are extraordinary even compared to other animals. There are many ways of describing these animals in the English language, and a type of adjective called a superlative is often used. 'The largest', for example, is one of these adjectives. Blue whales are the largest and the heaviest creatures in our oceans, and the largest and heaviest creatures on land are African elephants. Many other amazing animals are also native to the continent of Africa. Giraffes, for instance, are the tallest animals in the world, with the longest legs and necks, and ostriches are the largest and heaviest birds.

The fastest creature in the world is a bird called a peregrine falcon. These birds have been known to fly faster than 320 kilometres per hour, or 200 mph, which stands for 'miles per hour'. The fastest land animals are cheetahs, which can run at a speed of more than 96 kph, or 60 mph, and some of the slowest are tortoises. These very slow animals, though, have also lived the longest. In 1770 a British explorer called Captain Cook gave a tortoise to the Tongan royal family. It was alive in three centuries and died in 1965 at the age of at least 188. It was one of the oldest animals that has ever lived.

Find the right word(s) in the text above for each of the clues below:

1. The opposite of 'the youngest' (2 words)

2. The opposite of 'the lightest' (2 words)

3. The opposite of 'the fastest' (2 words)

4. The Atlantic and the Pacific

5. The rate at which someone or something can move

6. This can move even faster than a golden eagle (2 words)

7. Mammals that look like enormous fish

8. Animals with very long necks. They like eating acacia leaves

9. Animals that look like big cats and are yellow with black spots

10. Reptiles with large shells which cover most of their bodies

11. These birds can't fly, but they can run at over 40 mph

12. Have or use something with others, or at the same time as others

13. Periods of a hundred years

14. An adjective used to say animals (and plants) exist naturally in a place (2 words)

15. Someone who travels to new places to learn more about them

/ 15

106. Safaris, Zoos, and Farms

If you want to see wild animals in their natural habitat, one of the best places to visit is Africa. In most countries there are zoos, but the game reserves in African countries like Kenya and South Africa are much bigger than zoos, and the animals live freely in their natural environment. When they go on a safari to Africa, people usually want to see lions, leopards, buffaloes/buffalo, elephants and rhinos. These animals are known as the 'big five', not because of their size, but because in the past they were the most difficult and dangerous to hunt on foot. Although nowadays the 'big five' are protected in most reserves and should hopefully survive, the situation is very different elsewhere in Africa and other parts of the world. Poaching and the destruction of their environment have become serious problems for all five, and rhinos in particular are in danger of becoming extinct.

For most of us, the only places we see wild animals are on TV or in a zoo. Animals in zoos are kept in cages or enclosures behind glass windows so they can't escape, often in conditions which people consider cruel. Other animals are kept on farms, and while animal welfare is a serious issue for farm animals as well, organic farming has begun to make a real difference in the UK. For hundreds of years, farms have provided us with much of what we need in our daily lives. We get our dairy products from cows and goats, our eggs from hens, and our wool from sheep. Horses and pigs also live on farms, and while all of these animals are used for meat in some countries, more and more people have become vegetarian or vegan in recent decades.

Find the right word(s) in the text above for each of the clues below:

1. The well-being, health and safety of people and animals

2. A type of farming in which animals are free-range, and GM and other foods are prohibited

3. Another word for the natural environment of animals and plants

4. No longer in existence

5. An adjective used for actions which cause pain or suffering to people or animals

6. Illegal hunting of animals, birds or fish

7. Milk and cheese (2 words)

8. This is used to make clothes that keep us warm

9. Enormous animals with trunks and very large ears

10. Get away from a place that you usually can't leave

11. Continue to live or exist

12. Large, dangerous animals which are members of the cow family

13. Chase wild animals or birds to kill or capture them

14. We get cheese from cows and these other animals

15. An adjective used for animals that live in their natural environment and aren't tame

/ 15

107. Cats and Dogs

The only animals which are tame, rather than wild, are the ones that live with us at home as pets. Cats and dogs are the most popular pets in the world, and have been our companions for thousands of years. We become so fond of them that for many of us they're part of the family. Physically, cats and dogs are quite similar. Most of them have fur which covers their bodies. They all have four legs, paws with claws, tails, and warm, wet noses, but cats and dogs have very different personalities.

Cats are independent animals. Their territory is important to them, perhaps more important than other cats or people. Cats like to choose when to be with people. They tend to dislike being picked up, carried, and forced to sit on someone's lap.

Dogs are normally sociable animals. Since the time they hunted in packs they've always wanted to be with other dogs or humans. Most dogs love people moving towards them, patting them and playing with them. They need more attention and exercise than cats. Dogs like to go for regular walks with their owners, but cats have no interest in doing this. Unlike dogs, most are happy to be left at home during the day.

Cats and dogs enjoy playing different games. Cats love jumping on small moving objects, especially if they're attached to the end of a piece of string. Dogs like to fetch objects you've thrown for them. When they bring them back, some dogs drop them in front of you and others challenge you to pull them out of their mouths. Dogs are much easier to train than cats. Unlike cats, they learn to obey basic commands. If you tell a trained dog to 'sit', it sits. If you tell a cat to do something, it usually ignores you.

Find the right word(s) in the text above for each of the clues below:

1. An adjective used for animals that prefer to spend time with other animals, or people, than alone

2. Soft, thick hair that grows on some animals' bodies

3. Go and get something and bring it back

4. Held and taken from one place to another

5. This can be put round packages, and is used to tie things together

6. Sharp, curved nails at the end of an animal's or bird's foot

7. The feet of an animal that has nails or claws

8. Pays no attention to someone, (or something), or takes no notice of them

9. Chased other animals or birds to catch or kill them

10. Allow something to fall either on purpose or by accident

11. Physical activity which someone does to be fit, healthy or strong

12. Lifted off the floor, or collected from a place (2 words)

13. Orders given to a person or an animal

14. Groups of animals that hunt together

15. Touching something gently several times with a flat hand

/ 15

108. Birds

Scientists believe birds are descended from dinosaurs, those huge prehistoric animals which are now extinct. Unlike dinosaurs they probably survived because they have wings and can fly.

Birds have a lot of feathers, two wings and two legs. They also have a beak and warm blood, but they don't have any teeth. Most birds can fly, but some larger birds can't. Ostriches and emus can't fly, but they can run very fast. An ostrich has been known to run faster than a horse. Penguins can't fly either, but they can swim. When they're swimming in water they move their wings like other birds when they're flying!

Some species are very colourful. Flamingos / oes are bright pink and parrots are green, yellow, red and blue. Parrots are intelligent and can be very amusing. They can repeat words and phrases that humans say. Most birds are also sociable. They spend a lot of their time with other birds. They call and sing to each other and use a number of visual signals to communicate. The songs of male nightingales are some of the most beautiful sounds in nature. Many birds fly together in flocks and some travel thousands of miles when they migrate.

People put bird tables in their gardens so they can watch birds from their kitchen windows. They give them food and water, especially in the winter. Birdwatching is a popular hobby. We love to watch birds because they're beautiful and amazing creatures, but they need to be protected. There are at least 10,000 species of birds in the world, (and there may be as many as 18,000 according to some reports). A large number of these species, however, probably well over a thousand, are in danger of extinction.

Find the right word(s) in the text above for each of the clues below:

1. A red liquid that flows through the bodies of people, animals and birds

2. Small brown birds that sing at night and during the day

3. The feathers of these clever birds are a number of beautiful colours

4. A noun used for species of animal or bird that no longer exist

5. These birds are even bigger and faster than emus

6. Large black and white birds that live in the Antarctic. They've got wings, but they don't use them to fly

7. Groups of birds that are all the same kind and fly together

8. The hard part of a bird's mouth that sticks out

9. A word used for all living animals and birds

10. Dogs and cats are covered with fur, but birds' bodies are covered with these

11. Move from one part of the world to another

12. We use ours to chew food, but birds haven't got any of these

13. An adjective used for sight or something that is seen

14. This colour is a mixture of red and white

15. A group of animals or birds that are the same and reproduce with other members of the group

/ 15

109. Insects
....

Insects are much smaller than animals and birds. They've got six legs and their bodies are divided into three sections. They've also got long, thin parts on their heads, called antennae, which they use to touch and feel things. Most insects have wings and can fly, but some move around by walking as well, and others can even swim.

Insects can be annoying and some are dangerous. Mosquitos / oes are very common in hot countries. They bite humans and animals and drink their blood. When they do this our skin becomes itchy and uncomfortable. Prevent this by wearing long sleeves and trousers. There are sprays that mosquitos / oes don't like and creams you can use to stop the itching. Some flies bite as well, and horsefly bites are very unpleasant. Flies are dirty and, like mosquitos / oes, they can spread diseases. If you ever eat outside on a hot day, make sure they don't land on your plate or your food. Wasps like to fly around us too. They can be irritating, and if they sting you, it's painful. Some insects, like locusts, cause problems for farmers because they damage their crops. This is why farmers use pesticides to control and kill them. Other insects, called moths, damage our clothes. Put some mothballs in your drawers and wardrobes and they'll stay away.

Not all insects are a problem, though, and some are wonderful. Butterflies have wings that are beautiful colours. Bees provide us with honey, and silkworms, a type of moth, produce silk which is used to make ties, shirts and dresses.

Find the right word(s) in the text above for each of the clues below:

1.   Planes do this when they leave the air and arrive on the ground

2.   Snakes and mosquitoes do this

3.   If our skin feels like this we feel like scratching it

4.   These insects look like moths but most of them have more colourful wings

5.   These black and yellow insects sting and they don't make honey!

6. We want to do this when we're thirsty

7. Make sure something can't happen before it happens

8. An adjective used for anything that makes us slightly angry. It means the same as 'irritating'

9. These chemicals kill insects

10. Big insects that fly in large groups and destroy crops and plants

11. This is golden brown and we spread it on bread and toast like jam

12. We wear these parts of a shirt on our arms

13. Part of this insect's name is the same as an animal that people ride

14. Plants called nettles do this to us and so do wasps and bees

15. A verb which means 'harm' or 'ruin'

/ 15

110. Plants

A plant grows in the earth. Its roots spread outwards and downwards. They support the plant and give it water. All plants need water and light to grow. The part of the plant which grows above the earth is called the stem. Once the stem has grown the plant can produce leaves and flowers.

Trees are the largest plants in the world. The stem of a tree is called a trunk. Branches grow on the trunk and leaves grow on the branches. Some trees are evergreen which means they keep their leaves and they stay green through the different seasons. Other trees are deciduous. This means their leaves fall off in the autumn and new ones grow the following spring.

Plants are very important for human beings and animals. They remove harmful carbon dioxide from the air and turn it into oxygen which prevents global warming. We depend on them for food, especially for fruit and vegetables. We wouldn't have drinks like tea or coffee without plants and we get a lot of our medicines from plants, including aspirin. Many of the products we buy in shops come from plants. Anything made of plastic or rubber, for example. Soap, shampoo, paint and all our clothes made from cotton are also from plants, and what about the wood we get from trees? Wood is used to make buildings and boats, furniture and fences, paper and cardboard, as well as thousands of other things. Trees and other plants are so useful and important that we couldn't live without them.

Find the right word(s) in the text above for each of the clues below:

1. A plant can only grow above the earth if it's supported by these

2. These grow out from the trunk of a tree and from the stems of other large plants

3. Spring, summer, autumn and winter

4. A material like very thick paper which is used to make boxes

5. A gas which is in air and water. People, animals and plants can't live without it

6. This is used for pain relief

7. An adjective used to say that something can help you do what you want to do

8. A lot of clothes are made from this material

9. A liquid soap we use to wash our hair

10. The part of a plant that grows upwards above the roots

11. These are made of wood or metal and they separate a garden or a field from the one next to it

12. The stem of a large tree

13. Scientists think this gas causes global warming (2 words)

14. These float on water and transport people on lakes, rivers and at sea

15. This comes from a tropical plant and we make car tyres with it

/ 15

THE WORLD

111. Continents and Countries

There are seven large areas of land in the world which we call continents. Asia is the largest of these, followed by Africa, North America, South America, Antarctica, Europe and Australia. There are also far more people living in Asia than any other continent. It has a population of more than 4.5 billion people, six times the number of people living in Europe, and about 60% of the world's population.

Most continents have a number of countries in them. There are 54 countries in Africa, 50 in Europe and 48 countries in Asia. North America has 23 countries, including those in Central America, and South America has 12. The continent of Australia only has one country in it, which is Australia, so it's both a continent and a country, and Antarctica doesn't have any at all. Antarctica is further south than all the other continents and it's also the coldest, windiest and the least populated continent in the world. Nobody lives there permanently because it's almost completely covered by ice.

Russia is larger than any other country in the world. Although about a quarter of Russian land is in the continent of Europe, the other three quarters are in Asia. To give you an idea of how vast Russia is, its European part is the largest country in Europe. The second largest country in Europe is Ukraine, which is less than a fifth of the size. After Russia, the largest countries on our planet in order of their size or surface area are Canada, the US, China, Brazil, Australia and India.

Find the right word(s) in the text above for each of the clues below:

1.   Another way of writing 25%

2.   Another way of writing 20%

3.   Another way of writing 75% (2 words)

4.   This adverb is the opposite of 'temporarily'

5. We use this word to say how large or small something is

6. The opposite of 'the smallest' (2 words)

7. This means there are fewer people living there than any other place (3 words)

8. An adjective which means 'extremely large' or 'huge'

9. Parts of a place, town, country, continent or the world

10. Frozen water

11. The second largest continent

12. Spread over the whole surface of a place or an object

13. The largest country in North America

14. The largest country in South America

15. The second largest country in Asia

/ 15

112. Oceans

Salt water covers about 72% of the surface of our planet and almost all of this water is in our seas and five oceans. An ocean is a vast area of water between two continents. They are much larger than seas, and while our seas are partly or completely surrounded by land, our oceans are not. The world's oceans are also extremely deep. Their average depth is almost 3,700 metres. There are many forms of life in our oceans, and we depend on the fish and seafood that live in them. The creatures that live there are amazing, and some of the most wonderful are dolphins and whales. Dolphins are thought to be very intelligent and have been known to protect humans from sharks. Blue whales are bigger and heavier than anything else on our planet. One adult blue whale weighs about the same as 22 African elephants!

The largest ocean is the Pacific, which is west of North and South America, and east of Asia and Australia. It is so large that its surface area is greater than all the land in the world put together. The second largest is the Atlantic Ocean which is between the Americas, and Europe and Africa. After the Atlantic, the other oceans, in order of their size, are the Indian Ocean, the Southern Ocean and the Arctic Ocean. The Arctic Ocean is not only the smallest ocean, it's also the most northern and the shallowest.

Find the right word(s) in the text above for each of the clues below:

1. The fourth largest ocean in the world (3 words)

2. Animals that live in the sea and are often friendly towards humans

3. The flat top, exterior or outside of a place or an object

4. A word used to say how large or small something is

5. Prawns and crabs are two examples of this

6. Part of a place, town, country, continent or the world

7. Very large mammals that live in the sea and look like enormous fish

8. Large fish with sharp teeth. Some of them are very dangerous

9. The opposite of 'shallow'

10. We put a small amount of this in or on some of our food. It's also in our oceans and seas

11. This means the same as 'rely on' (2 words)

12. A verb which we use to say how heavy something is

13. Another way of saying 'combined' (2 words)

14. A word used for all living animals and birds

15. The third largest ocean in the world (3 words)

/ 15

113. Languages

English is spoken in more than a hundred countries in the world, more countries than any other language. More people also learn English as a foreign language than any other language, and it's widely considered to be the international business language. This is because millions of business people use it when they speak or write to native speakers of other languages, that is to say, people whose first language isn't English.

There are, however, two languages which are spoken by more native speakers in the world than English. Almost a billion people are native speakers of Mandarin, the main language in the north and the south west of China. After Mandarin, more people speak Spanish as a first language than any other. Spanish is spoken by about 400 million people, not only in Spain, but in most of South and Central America, and by Hispanic people in the United States. The language with the third largest number of native speakers in countries around the world is English. It's the main language in the UK, the US, Canada, Ireland, Australia and New Zealand. After English comes Hindi, which is the most common first language in India, a country with the largest population in the world. Arabic is next, with about 300 million native speakers, most of whom are in North Africa and the Middle East. Portuguese is also spoken as a first language by a large number of people. Did you know there are far more native speakers of Portuguese in Brazil than in Portugal?

Find the right word(s) in the text above for each of the clues below:

1. A country in South America where the main language isn't Spanish

2. This means the same as 'by a lot of people' or 'in many places'

3. A thousand million

4. All the people who live in a particular country, continent or the world

5. Connected with Spain, or originally from Spain but now in other countries as well

6. Thought to be (3 words)

7. The opposite of 'small'

8. More than 20% of the population of this country are native speakers of Bengali, Marathi or Telugu

9. About 60% of the people of this country are native speakers of English, and 20% are native speakers of French

10. Most Indian people are native speakers of this language

11. The first language of most people in Lisbon

12. The first language of most people in Argentina

13. The first language of most people in Egypt

14. The first language of more people than any other language

15. Making, buying, selling or supplying goods or services for money

/ 15

114. World Religions

In the UK and in most countries in the world, people are free to choose their religion. There are four main religions or beliefs in the world: Christianity, Islam, Hinduism and Buddhism. About a third of all believers are Christians, who believe in God and Jesus Christ. The Christians in Central and South America and Southern Europe are mainly Catholics, and the Christians in North America and Northern Europe are mostly Protestants. The main religion in the Middle East and North Africa is Islam. People who believe in Islam are called Muslims and most are either Sunni or Shia. They believe in Allah, who is their God, and the prophet, Muhammad, who lived more than 1,400 years ago. Hinduism, the third largest religion, is practised mainly in India, and has many different Gods.

Buddhists believe in a teacher called Buddha, but not in God. Most Buddhists live in East Asia and South East Asia. They practise meditation in silence by thinking deep thoughts and becoming very calm. In the three main religions, believers normally pray to God instead. There are also people who don't believe in God, who are called atheists, and people who don't know if God exists, who are called agnostics.

Find the right word(s) in the text above for each of the clues below:

1. People who feel certain or are confident that God exists or something is true

2. A person sent by God to teach people and give them messages from God

3. The pope is the religious leader of these people

4. People who are not sure whether there is a God

5. The main religion in Iraq, Iran, Egypt and Algeria

6. The main religion in Europe and the Americas

7. The main religion in Mumbai and Delhi

8. More than 90% of the people of Thailand

9. A word with a similar meaning to 'in the past'

10. People who believe God doesn't exist

11. These Christians separated from the Catholic Church in the 16th century

12. Quiet and relaxed, not upset or excited at all

13. No noise or sound

14. A verb used to say someone or something is real, living or present

15. A word that has a similar meaning to 'usually'

/ 15

115. Earth and Other Planets

The world we live in is a planet which is known as Earth. Earth is one of eight planets which orbit a star called the Sun. A group of planets and the star they move around is called a solar system, and ours is one of many solar systems in space. Each planet is the shape of a ball except Saturn which looks very different from the others. This is because it has rings around it which are made of ice and rock. The planets which are closest to Earth are Venus and Mars, and Earth has its own Moon, which goes round our planet. We see the Moon in the sky at night, and the Sun during the day. The Sun provides energy, and in particular, the heat and light that we need on Earth.

Life is only possible on planets that have water. A planet too close to its Sun would be too hot to have water on it. Any water would boil and turn into a gas. If a planet is too far away from its Sun, any water would freeze and become ice. Earth is the right distance from the Sun for life to exist on our planet. It's not too hot and not too cold. Although it's the only planet we know has life on it, it's possible there are other planets in other solar systems where some forms of life also exist. Any planet the same size as Earth and about the same distance from its Sun could have the right conditions for life.

Find the right word(s) in the text above for each of the clues below:

1. The opposite of 'furthest away from' (2 words)

2. A verb used to say someone or something is real, living or present

3. One of the planets nearest Earth, and the second smallest in our solar system after Mercury

4. One of the planets nearest Earth, and also the hottest in our solar system

5. A very hard, solid material that forms part of the surface of the Earth and other planets

6. What water would do at 100 degrees Celsius

7. What water would do at 0 degrees Celsius

8. A planet which is surrounded by rings

9. This means 'move around' or 'go around' a planet

10. How far one person, object or place is from another

11. Round or circular objects with holes in the middle

12. The area outside Earth's atmosphere where all the solar systems are

13. A formal word for 'gives'

14. Physical situations necessary for something to exist or happen

15. Oxygen and hydrogen are two examples of this

/ 15

116. Wars

Wars have been fought throughout history and have had many different causes. Some of the most terrible wars started when one country invaded another country with its army and tried to take control. There have also been civil wars, which happen when two or more groups of people from the same country fight against each other. The two World Wars in the 20th century were fought by a large number of countries. Battles were won and lost. Many different types of weapon were used, most of which were guns or bombs. Soldiers fought on foot and in tanks. Planes attacked each other in the air, and at sea, ships were sunk by submarines. Innocent civilians became the victims of war. In the two World Wars, more than a hundred million people were killed, wounded or died, and more than half of them were civilians.

Wars between countries and civil wars have continued in the 21st century, but there is some hope that a third World War will not happen and we can live in peace. Before nuclear weapons, governments and military leaders believed they could win a war. With nuclear weapons, countries at war are likely to destroy each other. The dangers are so great that a war with these weapons is not an option.

Find the right word(s) in the text above for each of the clues below:

1. During the whole period of something

2. An adjective used to describe people who haven't done anything wrong

3. A word which means 'take part in a battle or a war against an enemy'

4. People who have been hurt or who died in an accident, a crime, a war, or because of a disease

5. Walking (2 words)

6. A general word for anything used to attack or fight someone

7. A period of time when there is no war

8. Damage something so badly that it no longer exists

9. Damaged so badly that they went from the surface to the bottom of the ocean

10. Went into a country with soldiers to take control of it

11. People who are not in the army, the navy, the air force or the police

12. Hurt or injured by a weapon in a battle or a war

13. Weapons that explode

14. Fights between armies, ships or planes during a war

15. Ships that can travel underwater

/ 15

117. Poverty and Hunger

People who are poor have very little money and few possessions. They live in poverty. In some countries poverty is such a serious problem that people don't have enough food, clean water, or even clothes. They don't have good enough housing either, and many of them have to live without health care or education. There are about a billion people in the world who live in poverty without the everyday things that most of us have.

Some of the poorest people in the world live in Africa, in countries without enough agriculture or food to provide what people need. A few of these countries are mostly desert, where very little grows, and there isn't enough rain. The worst disasters happen, though, during a period of weather with no rain, which is called a drought. When there's a drought there's often little or no water or food. People who are very thirsty may drink dirty water which causes disease. Without food or water, they lose weight, become ill and are desperate for help. They are so hungry that they starve. International organisations provide aid as soon as they can, but much more could be done to help these people and save their lives. There are still millions of men, women and children who try to survive every day without clean water or enough to eat.

Find the right word(s) in the text above for each of the clues below:

1. Suffer or die because there isn't enough food to eat

2. A general word for places with walls and roofs that people live in

3. A large area of land, covered by sand, with little or no water

4. In extreme need of something and without hope

5. Drops of water that fall from the sky

6. A medical service with doctors and nurses, treatment and medicines (2 words)

7. Things that people own or that belong to them

8. Growing crops on farms and farming

9. The state of being poor

10. Illness or sickness that humans or animals suffer from, and can kill plants

11. How someone feels when they need or want to drink

12. How someone feels when they need or want to eat

13. Continue to live in a difficult or dangerous situation

14. Very bad situations, events or accidents that can result in death or destruction

15. Food, medicines, money or anything else which is sent to help people

/ 15

118. Disasters
....

In a famine or a drought, people die because there isn't enough food or water. Other disasters happen when there's too much water. There are floods after days or weeks of heavy rain. Rivers and seas are so full that they flood the land. Houses and roads are under water which causes terrible damage to property. Towns and villages are cut off and have no food or electricity until emergency aid arrives.

Unlike floods, some disasters are unexpected and sudden. Accidents, fires and earthquakes all happen suddenly. An air or road accident, or an accident at sea can happen in a few seconds. Fires spread so quickly through buildings and dry areas of land that they are soon out of control. If there's a serious earthquake in a city or a large town, buildings collapse and people are injured and killed. An earthquake under the sea produces giant waves which are called tsunamis. When they reach the coast, people drown and buildings are destroyed. There was a tsunami in the Indian Ocean in December 2004. Many of the people who lived or were on holiday next to the ocean were killed.

After a disaster there is sometimes an epidemic. This can happen when serious diseases spread in disaster areas. A lot of people may become ill and die unless they receive the right medical help.

Find the right word(s) in the text above for each of the clues below:

1. Floods, accidents, fires and earthquakes

2. A disaster that happens because there isn't enough food for people to eat

3. A disaster that happens because there isn't enough water for people to drink

4. The houses, land or possessions that people own or that belong to them

5. Help that people get in a very dangerous or serious situation (2 words)

6. This is what happens to buildings when they break apart and fall down

7. How people die if they are underwater for too long and can't breathe

8. Large amounts of water that cover an area which is normally dry

9. Houses, schools, churches and office blocks are all examples of these

10. Separated from the outside world (2 words)

11. A car crash (2 words)

12. This happens when the ground suddenly moves and shakes violently

13. Very quickly and unexpectedly

14. Affect more and more people or cover a larger and larger area

15. Damaged so badly that it no longer exists or works

/ 15

119. Climate Change

Climate change is about changes in the weather that happen over long periods of time. It's caused by natural processes like the heat that comes from the Sun. It's also caused by the movement of rock on the Earth's surface, and mountains called volcanos / oes when they erupt. Not all the changes are natural, though. Some human activities have caused changes in our climate and these changes are known as global warming.

Humans and animals breathe out a gas called carbon dioxide and we produce the same gas when we burn fossil fuels. The main fossil fuels are coal, oil and natural gas. We burn these fuels in cars and planes, in factories and in our homes. We burn them to make a huge number of products that we use every day. We also cut down trees and destroy forests all over the world. When we do all these things, carbon dioxide goes into the air and causes global warming. This has happened much more in the last hundred years than it did in previous centuries. Our land and oceans are getting warmer. Our icebergs are melting and sea levels are rising. There's more very bad weather like heatwaves, droughts and storms. There are more deserts as well, and animals and plants are dying because of the changes in temperature. It's a serious global problem.

Find the right word(s) in the text above for each of the clues below:

1. Long periods when there's little or no rain

2. Take air in and out of our lungs through our noses or mouths

3. A very hard material that is part of the Earth's surface

4. Large buildings where things are made

5. This is a black fossil fuel which is found under the ground

6. The Titanic hit one of these before it sank

7. Many of these hot, dry places are covered with sand

238

8. There are far more trees in these than there are in our woods

9. These produce heat and gases when they burn (2 words)

10. The measurement in degrees of how hot or cold somewhere or something is

11. When volcanoes do this, gases and hot liquid rock, (lava), are forced out of an opening at the top

12. This fossil fuel is a thick liquid

13. Periods of weather that are much hotter than normal

14. Changing from a solid form to a liquid form

15. Periods of very bad weather, with strong winds and heavy rain

/ 15

120. The Environment

Governments and large companies can do a lot to protect the environment and there are plenty of ways you and I can help as well. When we're at home we could save electricity by switching off most of the lights and other electrical appliances. We'd use less gas if we turned down the central heating or turned off the radiators. Why not have a shower instead of a bath, or use less water when we brush our teeth?

We could try not to throw our rubbish away. Most of it can be recycled. We ought to recycle all our paper and glass. Let's stop buying plastic bags, cups, bottles and cans. If we each had a bag, a cup and a bottle, we'd be able to use them again and again. We could easily read the news online, so we don't need to buy newspapers.

Food is transported thousands of miles, which causes pollution and wastes resources. We can buy food that's produced nearby, or has come from the farm down the road. Think of all the things we no longer use or need. Clothes, books and all those old things in the attic. Let's take them all to a recycling bank or a charity shop. Why do we have to drive to work every day when we could leave our cars at home and take public transport instead? These are all ways we can stop wasting things, and help to protect the environment. Let's see how many ideas we can put into action.

Find the right word(s) in the text above for each of the clues below:

1. The natural world which people, animals and plants live in (2 words)

2. We put this in our bins or take it to be recycled

3. Take care of something or look after it so it isn't in danger

4. This is a small room at the top of a house. It's also called a loft

5. Washing machines, hairdryers and lights are all examples of these (2 words)

6. Supermarkets give or sell these to us and we put our shopping in them (2 words)

7. We use a toothbrush and toothpaste to do this to our teeth

8. Hot water that goes from a boiler through pipes and radiators provides us with this at home (2 words)

9. A type of energy that's used in lights

10. Metal containers that we drink out of

11. Take things away and reproduce them so they can be used again

12. Uses something badly

13. Close to where something is

14. Clothes and other things are sold here to help people in need (2 words)

15. Carried or moved from one place to another by road, rail, sea, or air

/ 15

THE WEATHER

121. Words for Weather

There are lots of different words in the English language to describe the weather. When we talk about how hot or cold the weather is, it's to do with the temperature. When it's extremely cold we describe the weather as freezing. As the temperature rises above freezing, we might say it's very cold, then cold, then chilly and finally it becomes mild. Mild weather isn't really either hot or cold, but we tend to use the word for a winter's day which doesn't feel cold. At other times of the year when it's colder than we expect it to be, we often say it's not very warm. When temperatures are higher, for example in April or May, we say that it's warm, and in the summer months it can be hot. The temperature in the UK doesn't normally go above 30 degrees Celsius, but when it does some people describe it as boiling or baking.

A number of different words are used to talk about the wind and the rain as well. In the UK we don't have extreme enough weather to experience serious hurricanes or tornados / oes, but we do have gales and strong winds. Windy weather is usually unpleasant, but a gentle breeze, especially on a hot day, can be refreshing and pleasant. The words we use for rain are to do with how much rain there is. When it's been raining but it's stopped we say it's wet or it feels damp. Light rain is frequently called drizzle and a short period of rain is a shower. Heavy rain can be described as a downpour, and some of us use the expressions 'it's pouring with rain', and 'it's raining cats and dogs'!

Find the right word(s) in the text above for each of the clues below:

1. Extremely hot, or a type of cooking (without any oil) in an oven

2. An adjective used for anything that makes us feel less hot or tired

3. Not very cold, but too cold to be comfortable

4. Violent storms with very strong winds, mostly at sea

5. When there's a tornado, these move in circles

6. Zero degrees Celsius or colder

7. A light wind

8. Weather which is pleasant because it isn't as cold as we expected

9. Extremely hot, or water at 100 degrees Celsius

10. The opposite of 'lower'

11. The opposite of 'started'

12. A noun used for rain that's falling heavily

13. An adjective used for weather that's between mild and hot

14. Slightly wet and not very pleasant

15. Strong winds, but less strong than hurricanes or tornadoes

/ 15

122. What Weather!

British people love to complain about the weather. A study found that each of us mentions or talks about the weather an average of four times a day! We spend more time talking about the weather than any other subject. We let people know we're unhappy when we think it's too cold, or when the skies are grey and it's cloudy. We do the same when it rains and it's windy, and if it's icy we worry we might slip and fall, so we tell each other to be careful. If we get soaked in the rain or we're freezing cold, that's all we want to talk about. We even complain on the few days every year when it's too hot.

At other times, though, we really can be positive about the weather. When there are blue skies and it's warm, we love to talk about it. When it's cold and raining outside, and we're sitting in a warm room at home, we tell each other how cosy it feels. We can't resist talking about unusual weather either. Storms are exciting, so we enjoy talking about them. When we hear thunder or see lightning we can't wait to tell someone. Snow's exciting too, especially when it's going to snow heavily, so we let each other know. We love to predict the weather and tell people what the forecast has predicted, so we do that as well. In fact, we enjoy talking about the weather so much it's often the first thing we mention!

Find the right word(s) in the text above for each of the clues below:

1. A verb used to say what we think is going to happen

2. Periods of very bad weather with strong winds and heavy rain

3. An adjective that describes the weather when air moves quickly

4. An adjective that describes the weather when water has frozen

5. An adjective that describes the weather when there are grey or white formations of water in the sky

6. Very loud noises during storms

7.   Very bright lights in the sky during storms

8.   Small, soft, white pieces of frozen water that fall from the sky

9.   Clouds, the sun, the moon and the stars appear in these

10. A word which describes people or clothes that are very wet

11. Hotter than mild, but less hot than hot!

12. Warm and comfortable

13. A TV, radio or website report with information about today's, tomorrow's and this week's weather

14. Zero degrees Celsius or colder

15. Say we're unhappy about, or not satisfied with, something

/ 15

123. The Four Seasons

Spring in the UK is a season with a mixture of different types of weather. In March the weather can be cold and wet and it sometimes snows. April is known for its showers, but it's normally one of the driest months of the year. Most years there isn't much rain in May either, and we notice the days are drier and warmer. During spring, (but with climate change in many cases before), flowers appear and birds start building their nests. The days become longer.

Summer is from June until August and is warmer and sunnier than the other seasons. It also has longer days. This is because the UK is in a part of the world that faces the sun in the summer months, so more sunshine and daylight reaches us. In London on the 21st of June sunrise is at 4.42am and sunset is at 9.20pm. It's usually the longest day of the year with more than sixteen hours of daylight.

Autumn lasts from September to November. It's an unsettled period, which can be cold and wet at times, and there are likely to be more storms than at any other time of year. Flowers die and leaves go brown and fall from the trees. Some autumns the weather stays warm during the day until October, and even the nights are mild. This is known as an Indian Summer.

December, January and February are winter months. Winter is the coldest, wettest and windiest season. Towards the end of winter there is usually less wind and rain, but it becomes even colder and it often snows. It also begins with the shortest days of the year. In London on the 21st of December sunrise is just after 8am and sunset is just before 4pm. It's usually the shortest day of all with about eight hours of daylight.

Find the right word(s) in the text above for each of the clues below:

1. Periods of sixty minutes

2. Short periods of rain

3. The last month of spring

4. The first month of summer

5. The second month of autumn

6. The third month of winter

7. Less wet

8. Not as cold as expected

9. The time of day when it becomes light

10. The time of day when it becomes dark

11. A superlative adjective used for the lowest temperatures (2 words)

12. An adjective used for weather that changes a lot

13. A verb used for small, soft, white pieces of frozen rain when they fall from the sky

14. The light and heat of the sun

15. Periods of very bad weather with strong winds and heavy rain

/ 15

124. Extreme Weather

Of all the continents on Earth, North America, and in particular the United States, has the greatest variety of extremely bad weather conditions, which we often describe as extreme weather. This is mainly due to its location, about halfway between the equator and the North Pole, as well as having the Pacific Ocean to the west and the Atlantic to the east. Cold, dry air from Canada meets the warm tropical air from the oceans and the Gulf of Mexico, which causes the extreme weather. The continent doesn't have a mountain range from west to east that could prevent this from happening.

As a result, the US has every type of weather from droughts to blizzards. It has more than a thousand tornados / oes a year, (or 80% of those on the planet), mostly in central and south eastern regions, and ten times as many thunderstorms. There are also heatwaves, wildfires, hurricanes, torrential rain and floods. These extreme forms of weather cause destruction and loss of life throughout the year as they move across the country. Europeans who arrived in the US hundreds of years ago were shocked by the weather they experienced compared to weather in Europe. Although weather forecasts now warn Americans and Canadians of the dangers, extreme weather is still a serious problem across the continent.

Find the right word(s) in the text above for each of the clues below:

1.   An adverb which has a similar meaning to 'very seriously'

2.   TV, radio or website reports with information about today's, tomorrow's or this week's weather

3.   An imaginary line around the middle of the earth

4.   Falling very heavily or in large amounts

5.   Stop something before it can happen

6.   Violent storms with very strong winds, mostly at sea

7. One more than nine hundred and ninety-nine

8. Feeling very surprised by something, (which is usually unpleasant)

9. Snowstorms with very strong winds

10. This is what people breathe in hot countries (2 words)

11. Large amounts of water which cover areas that should be dry

12. Long periods (of time) when there is little or no rain

13. Periods of very bad weather with heavy rain, thunder and lightning

14. Periods of extremely hot weather

15. Damage which is so bad that something no longer exists

/ 15

125. The Forecast

"Good morning. Today in the UK the weather will start very cold and frosty for many of us, with some icy patches, especially in the south east. The ice will cause dangerous driving conditions, so if you're driving today, please take care. As the day progresses, it will be mainly dry with some sunny spells, but there will be wintry showers around the coasts, particularly in Wales and South West England. Temperatures are unlikely to rise above five degrees Celsius. During the evening, sleet and snow will spread into north western areas, where there may well be several centimetres of snow. Elsewhere it will be dry but with the probability of a widespread frost developing. It will be cloudy overnight with some scattered showers.

Tuesday will bring more showers, mostly in the west, but elsewhere it should be a relatively dry day. It will feel very cold in the wind, which is likely to get stronger later on, especially in the afternoon. The outlook for Wednesday, Thursday and Friday is much improved with rising temperatures and only a chance of isolated showers. It will feel milder, with daytime temperatures as high as eleven or twelve Celsius, although the nights will be cold. It's expected to be drier than the first half of the week, with less rain, but the possibility of snow showers on higher ground in the north of England and Scotland."

Find the right word(s) in the text above for each of the clues below:

1. This country is to the west of England

2. This country is to the north of England

3. Less cold than expected

4. Move or go up

5. Showers that are spread far apart over a large area

6. Small, icy areas which are separated from others around them

7. The opposite of 'low'

8. This means 'separated' from other showers

9. Spread over a wide area

10. A formal word for the weather we're likely to have for the rest of the week

11. Not wet

12. Areas of land next to the sea

13. Thin layers of ice on the ground and other surfaces, especially at night

14. A mixture of rain and snow

15. Frozen water

/ 15

MONEY AND FINANCE

126. Money and Currencies

Before you visit another country, find out as much as you can about the money used there. If the country you're going to has the same currency as your country, you won't need to change your money. It would be useful, though, to learn how expensive it is compared to your country. Many European countries have the euro, but if you're travelling from one of these countries to the UK, you may be asked whether you'd like to pay for something in euros or pounds sterling. If you choose to use your debit or credit card, but to withdraw an amount of money in the local currency as well, bear in mind that some banks and organisations offer better exchange rates than others. If you do some research and compare different rates you could save some money.

In South America, Argentina, Chile, Colombia and Uruguay all have the peso as their currency, and English-speaking countries, like Australia, Canada, the US and New Zealand, use the dollar. China has the yuan, Japan has the yen, Russia the rouble and South Africa the rand. There are lots of other currencies, too, and you can always find this information online. Finding out about their notes and coins would also help you. Using numbers instead of words, in the UK there are 50, 20, 10 and 5 pound notes and the coins are worth 1 pound, 50p, (which is short for 'pence'), 20p, 10p, 5p, 2p and 1p. If you're planning to visit the UK, see what they look like online and check how large or small and what shape they are. It will be easier to recognise and count them when you're here !

Find the right word(s) in the text above for each of the clues below:

1. Triangular, circular and square are three examples of this

2. Use these to calculate how much you'll get if you change your money into a different currency (2 words)

3. An adjective that's used to say how valuable something is

4. These pieces of paper are used as money

5. These small metal objects are used as money

6. This is the main currency used in London (2 words)

7. This is the main currency used in Tokyo

8. The peso, dollar, pound and euro are all examples of these

9. Know what something is because you've seen it before

10. Do this to find out and learn as much as you want about something

11. The currency in Germany, France, Italy and Spain

12. The main currency in Buenos Aires

13. Look at something carefully to make sure you know what it is

14. Calculate the total number or amount of something

15. Examine two or more things to see how similar or different they are

/ 15

127. Bank Accounts

Before you choose which bank to join, talk to friends and read as much as you can online. Banks offer different accounts which pay different amounts of interest and many offer other benefits that could be useful, like travel insurance. You can open most of them online or by calling the bank. Some banks and building societies require you to go into your local branch to have a meeting with one of their advisers /ors. They may also ask you to bring an identity card, passport, driving licence or household bill to prove who you are.

You can normally choose to have a current account and a savings account. It's likely that the interest rates you receive will be different for each account. Interest rates are calculated as a percentage of the amount of money you have in your account. So if you have a thousand pounds and the interest rate is one 1%, the interest you will earn after a year will be ten pounds.

A bank may also give you an overdraft allowance. This means they let you spend more money, or get more money out of a cash machine, than you have in your account. This is called being overdrawn or in debit. If you've got some money in your account you are in credit. Banks charge much higher interest rates if you are overdrawn than you receive for being in credit, so be careful. Find out exactly what their interest rates are before you open any account!

Find the right word(s) in the text above for each of the clues below:

1. Show that something is true

2. These are similar to banks. Customers can have current and savings accounts with them (2 words)

3. We keep money in these at a bank or building society

4. A percentage offered to customers by banks and building societies (2 words)

5. An account for day to day spending (2 words)

6. An account for people who want to save their money (2 words)

7. This is what you are if you're overdrawn or you owe the bank money (2 words)

8. This is what you are if you've got some money in your account (2 words)

9. Most banks and building societies in the UK have more than one that you can visit

10. A word with ten letters that we use for the symbol %

11. If the bank arranges this for you, you can take out more money than you have in your account (2 words)

12. Money you earn for staying in credit

13. Use money to buy or pay for something

14. This pays for the cost of any loss or damage to your property, or the cost of treatment if you're sick

15. Things that are helpful to you or good for you

/ 15

128. Earning Money

If you get a job in the UK you'll be given wages or a salary and your employment contract should say how much this is. There is a minimum wage and you can check the exact amount online. You should earn at least this amount per hour, and hopefully more. Wages are paid for manual jobs, like working in a bar or a restaurant, and are usually paid weekly. Salaries are paid to office workers or people who work at desks. These are paid monthly. A salary is also normally a number in pounds for a year's work, so it's an annual amount. If you receive a salary, you'll need a bank account so that money can be transferred to your account every month. If you're paid wages then you may receive your payment in cash. Keep any information you get on your monthly or weekly payments. You may need this when you pay tax or complete a tax return at the end of the financial year. The financial or tax year is from the beginning of April to the end of March the following year.

Inflation is a word we use to say how much the cost of living goes up from one month to the next, so things in the shops become more expensive because of inflation. In some jobs people get a salary or wages increase once a year so they can afford to buy food and pay for their rent, transport and other costs. If you're good at your job and you work hard, you might get a promotion at work. If you do, you should get a higher salary or an increase in your wages so you're earning the right amount for your new job.

Find the right word(s) in the text above for each of the clues below:

1. This means the same as 'rises' (2 words)

2. A rise in the amount or number of something

3. Have enough money to buy or pay for something

4. Cars, buses and trains

5. Money paid by a tenant to a landlord

6. Money in the form of notes and coins

7. Money we earn that goes to the government, who decide what to spend it on

8. This word means 'next'

9. The opposite of 'maximum'

10. An adverb which means 'with a lot of effort'

11. Moved from one place to another place

12. A move into a more important, senior or better paid job

13. All the important details about your job are in this document (2 words)

14. This document is used to calculate how much tax you owe (2 words)

15. These are like tables with drawers. People sit at them and do their work

/ 15

129. Spending Money

It's very easy to spend more money than you earn, which means you'll end up in debt. Owing other people money or being overdrawn at your bank can be a serious financial problem. It's always best to avoid having these problems. A good way of doing this is to have a budget. On the first day of the month, on your laptop or a piece of paper, make a list of all the things that you need to pay for or buy during the month. Next to each item, type or write down how much it will cost. When you've finished, compare what you're going to spend with the money you're going to earn and the amount you have in your bank account. Check what you've spent at the end of every week, and make sure you spend less than you earn.

You may be offered a credit card by your bank. A credit card is okay as long as you pay back what you owe every month. Be careful, though. If you forget, or don't have enough money to pay your credit card bill, you'll have to pay a large amount of interest to the bank. If you choose a debit card instead, you'll only be able to spend what you have in your account, or up to the maximum of an overdraft allowance agreed with your bank. You may find it easier to control your spending with a debit card than a credit card. Try to stay in credit if you can. If you owe your bank money you may be offered a loan to pay back what you owe. Like being overdrawn, though, you'll have to pay a lot of interest to the bank, so it could be very expensive.

Find the right word(s) in the text above for each of the clues below:

1. The amount of money someone has to spend on something, and a plan of how it will be spent

2. Having some money in your account (2 words)

3. This card only lets you spend the money you've got in your account (2 words)

4. Money you earn from the bank, or the bank charges you for being overdrawn

5. The opposite of 'cheap'

6. Examine two or more things to see how similar or different they are

7. What you are if you spend more money than you have in your account without permission

8. An amount of money that a bank lends someone

9. Try not to do something

10. Used money to buy or pay for something

11. A verb used for an obligation to pay some money

12. If you're in this situation, you owe people money (2 words)

13. A piece of paper which tells you how much you owe for a particular service, or a meal in a restaurant

14. A type of allowance which lets you spend more money than you have in your account (2 words)

15. The opposite of 'started'

/ 15

130. Gambling

In the UK, spending money on games of chance is legal, and about a third of the population play the lottery or take part in some form of gambling every month. Some people visit a casino from time to time to play roulette or cards for money, and others go to betting shops. Horse racing used to be the main sport for gambling, but nowadays people can risk their money on almost anything to do with chance. There are so many ways to gamble online that more and more people are winning and losing their money at home. They choose to play online games or to bet on sports which are live. Instead of travelling to a particular sports event, they can watch sport live on their TVs, their computers and phones. It's never been easier to place a bet.

Gambling a few pounds every now and again can be fun, but spending and losing much larger amounts of money causes serious problems. For people who are unable to control their gambling, it's a type of addiction, like being addicted to drugs or alcohol. The more money they lose, the more desperate they become to win it back. When they run out of their own money, they may steal money to carry on gambling. Apart from financial problems, the addiction can also result in crime and destroy relationships. It can cause depression and anxiety. Help, however, is available. If gamblers accept they have a problem and decide to do something about it, there are organisations that can help them to stop.

Find the right word(s) in the text above for each of the clues below:

1. The possibility of something happening

2. Any televised or online sport or event that's happening as you watch it

3. An activity which is illegal, (against the law)

4. An adjective used to say it's possible to have or receive something

5. A habit which is so serious that someone can't stop doing it

6. A game played with a ball, a moving wheel, and 39 numbers

7.   Blackjack and poker are two examples of this type of game

8.   This word has a similar meaning to 'gamble'

9.   Take someone else's money without their knowledge or permission

10. The winning numbers in this game are announced on TV, radio and online

11. People go online or go to this place to gamble on roulette and blackjack

12. Put your money or something valuable in a situation where it could be lost

13. The state of feeling worried and nervous

14. The state of feeling sad and hopeless

15. Needing or wanting something so much that someone will do almost anything to get it

/ 15

131. Meat

I've eaten meat all my life. In recent years, though, I've become more concerned that animals have to suffer and die for us to eat meat. I've also read that meat can be bad for our health. Eating meat, or at least some meat, is thought to increase the chances of cancer and heart disease. Processed meat, like bacon, sausage and ham, may be worse for us than other meat. Red meat could be less healthy than white meat, and both are less healthy than fish.

I've decided I should probably no longer eat processed or red meat. This would mean no more cooked breakfasts or ham sandwiches for lunch at work. I've always eaten beef, so I would have to give up roast beef, steak, stews and minced meat. The other red meat I've often had is lamb, so I would stop eating roast lamb and chops. Chicken and pork are the only white meats that I've eaten regularly. I've enjoyed duck and turkey as well, but I don't have them very often. I've tended only to eat duck two or three times a year, and turkey just once, on Christmas day!

I never thought I'd give up eating meat altogether, but in the last few months something has changed. I've been buying vegetarian sausages for a while now, but more recently I've started eating a wide variety of other foods that no longer contain meat, including burgers, steaks, cottage pies and lasagne. I've realised for the first time in my life that I could, and probably should, become a vegetarian. I'm concerned about animal welfare and, as I get older, I'm more concerned about my own health, and what's good for me. Vegetarian and vegan food is now widely available in supermarkets and shops, and it tastes so much better than it used to years ago. There are plenty of reasons why it makes sense to stop eating meat, and it's never been easier to do.

Find the right word(s) in the text above for each of the clues below:

1. A general word for meat that comes from a cow

2. The word we use for a young sheep and the meat that comes from it

3. Meat which hasn't been processed and comes from a pig

4. Feel pain or experience something unpleasant

5. I've eaten meat from this bird less often than chicken but more often than turkey

6. A thick slice of beef which can be eaten rare, medium rare, or well done

7. A verb used for our experience of eating something, (to do with one of our senses)

8. Meat that's been changed, often by adding salt, so it can be kept for longer

9. An adjective used to describe meat which has been cut into very small pieces using a machine

10. An adjective used for food cooked with oil in an oven

11. Meat and vegetables cooked slowly in a liquid

12. This food is a mixture of meat from a pig, fat, and bread

13. Full English breakfasts are cooked meals which normally include eggs, sausages and this other meat from a pig

14. Pasta available either with minced beef, or as a vegetarian dish

15. Thick slices of meat which are cooked with the bone attached to them

/ 15

132. Fish and Seafood

Some of the best fresh fish in the UK are served in fish and chip shops and restaurants on the coast. The fishing boats arrive with their catch early in the morning, and by lunchtime the same day, the fish appear in local towns, on menus and plates, or wrapped in paper to take away. In fish and chip shops there's often a choice of cod, haddock or plaice, fried in batter, (which is a mixture of eggs, milk and flour), but a much wider variety of fresh fish is available elsewhere. Turbot, sea bass, sole, and halibut, for example, are served in fish and seafood restaurants, and there's a great deal of fresh fish to choose from in fishmongers' shops and some supermarkets. Tinned fish, though, is sold in supermarkets in large quantities, and tinned tuna, salmon, and sardines can be found in almost any shop selling food in tins. Most of us prefer fish that's freshly cooked, but there are good reasons to buy tinned fish as well. It can be kept at home as long as you want, it's rich in healthy oils, and it's relatively cheap.

Other fish can be bought frozen in shops and supermarkets. A popular frozen food, especially for children, is fish fingers, which are smaller pieces of fish covered in breadcrumbs. Fishcakes, which are round pieces of fish mixed with potato, are also covered in breadcrumbs and can be bought either fresh or frozen. Another frozen food that people buy and is covered in either breadcrumbs or batter, is scampi, or Dublin Bay prawns. Eating prawns as scampi is only one of many ways to enjoy prawns, though. They're the most popular seafood in both the UK and the US, (in the US they're called shrimps), mainly because they're so versatile. Prawns are delicious in garlic, with spaghetti, rice or noodles, in salads, soups and curries, with avocado, and numerous other foods. Other seafood options include fresh crab, scallops, mussels and oysters, which are served in restaurants across the world. We only eat them at home on special occasions, because they take time to prepare and can be expensive, but they're much less expensive than lobster!

Find the right word(s) in the text above for each of the clues below:

1. Covered in paper or some other material

2. Metal containers

3. 'Dover' and 'Lemon' are two types of this fish

4. Make food ready, so it can be eaten

5. A noun used for fish that are caught

6. Having many different uses

7. Fish that may be named after an island in the Mediterranean

8. When it's alive this sea creature has a hard shell and claws, and moves sideways on land

9. A white powder which is used to make bread and cakes, and cook fried fish

10. In France and Belgium these are known as 'moules'

11. Very tasty

12. These fish swim up rivers to lay their eggs

13. In Scotland it's usually the fish in a 'fish supper'

14. Liked or enjoyed by a large number of people

15. This seafood comes in a shell. In restaurants it's normal to have either six or twelve of them on a plate

/ 15

133. Vegetables

Vegetables are very good for us. They're full of vitamins and protect us from serious diseases, so they're an important part of a healthy diet. We don't usually eat one vegetable on its own, though, because most of us enjoy them much more when we have them with other vegetables or food. Salads are a good example. Lettuce doesn't taste of much without anything else, but adding other vegetables makes a big difference. Try it with chopped onions and peppers, some small tomatoes, cucumber, and a salad dressing. You'll probably enjoy it more.

Vegetables go well with other foods too. Have you tried chicken with carrots and sprouts, or fish with new potatoes and peas? Another dish I would recommend is steak in a peppercorn sauce with mushrooms and spinach, and cauliflower and cheese are such a good combination there's a dish called cauliflower cheese! What about green beans and broccoli? They're tasty as part of almost any cooked dish served hot, but they're enjoyable cold as well, especially in salads on a warm day. In the winter, though, when it's cold, why not use the vegetables in your fridge or larder to make a hot vegetable soup?

There are hundreds of different ways of eating vegetables. Just ask a vegetarian!

Find the right word(s) in the text above for each of the clues below:

1. Green leaves that we cook and eat hot, or add to a salad and eat cold

2. Baked, broad and green are three types of this vegetable

3. Vegetables that are round and either light or dark brown, or white

4. The word for this vegetable is easier to spell if you remember it has two 'c's and one 'l'

5. Vegetables that are normally bright red, yellow, green or orange

6. These are in vegetables and other food. They're invisible, but they're good for us

7. A mixture of different vegetables, usually eaten cold

8. Mix olive oil with vinegar to make this (2 words)

9. Orange vegetables that are long and pointed

10. This vegetable has large, light green leaves and is used for salads

11. Two or more things that are mixed, joined or put together

12. A vegetable with dark green skin that we cut into thin slices and eat cold

13. The long name for these vegetables starts with the same letters as the capital of Belgium!

14. A large, round, white vegetable with green leaves around it

15. These tiny, round vegetables are usually sold frozen in bags

/ 15

134. Fruit

Preparing a fruit salad for a large family doesn't take long. First of all, choose your favourite fruit and buy it from your local market, greengrocer's or supermarket. Wash all the fruit in cold water before you start to prepare it.

This is a recipe I made up recently for my family, but you can put any fruit you like in a fruit salad.

Take a pineapple and cut off the top and the bottom of the fruit. Carefully remove the thick skin before cutting it into smaller chunks. (Chunks are thick pieces of food). Peel seven oranges, divide two of them into segments, (the small parts of a piece of fruit), and cut the segments in half. When you've done this, take the skin off two apples and a melon, and cut them into smaller chunks, but make sure you take out the middle parts and the pips. Now slice two peaches into smaller pieces and remove the stones from the middle of the fruit, before cutting some cherries in half and taking their stones out as well. The next thing to do is to slice some grapes and strawberries into two or three pieces. To make the juice, squeeze the five oranges that are left into a large bowl and add about the same amount of water, before putting all the fruit in as well.

Raspberries, pears, and kiwifruit are three other fruit you might want to include. Be careful with bananas, though. They lose their colour and go brown and mushy if they're left in the juice for too long, so put them in at the last minute! Finally, when you serve your fruit salad, why not add some yogurt / yoghurt / yoghourt, and put a spoonful of honey on top?

Find the right word(s) in the text above for each of the clues below:

1. Soft, red fruit that are often eaten with cream, and are larger than cherries and raspberries

2. Long, yellow fruit with yellow skin

3. A tropical fruit that can be eaten on its own, in a fruit salad, and even as a topping on a pizza!

4. Wine is made from these fruit

5. Fruit that are similar to nectarines

6. Honeydew and Cantaloupe are two types of this fruit, which is often eaten with Parma ham

7. Small, dark red fruit with stones in the middle

8. The small, hard seeds in apples, lemons, grapes and melons

9. These fruit are green, red or yellow. You can peel them or eat them with the peel on

10. Red fruit that are smaller than strawberries, and softer than cherries

11. Fruit with green skin. They're about the same size and shape as hens' eggs.

12. Make food ready, so it can be eaten

13. Press hard on a fruit with your hands so that juice comes out of it

14. A deep, round dish that we put liquids or food into

15. A shop that only sells fruit and vegetables

/ 15

135. Drinks

There are plenty of soft drinks in shops and supermarkets and many of them are bad for us. Most fizzy drinks and energy drinks have a lot of sugar in them. It's a good idea to check how much sugar there is by reading the label. If you buy fizzy drinks, it's best to choose diet ones. There's also sugar in drinks like orange squash and orange juice. At home and at school, most children drink milk. Adults drink a lot of coffee and tea at home and at work. At night before they go to bed people usually have warm milk, hot chocolate, or herbal teas such as camomile / chamomile, and peppermint. Herbal teas help us relax and have a good night's sleep.

Alcoholic drinks are available almost everywhere. Pubs and bars sell different types of beer. In the UK customers can order a pint or half a pint of lager or bitter. There's sweet or dry cider and a choice of white, red or rosé wines. There are spirits too, like whisky, rum and vodka. Spirits are very strong, though, because they have high alcoholic content, so it's dangerous to drink too much of them. Choose a cocktail instead. Cocktails are normally a mixture of spirits and soft drinks like fruit juice. Better still, drink water! In most bars and restaurants you can ask for still or sparkling water in bottles, or tap water. To stay healthy we need to drink water every day. Women are advised to drink at least one and a half litres a day, and men as much as two litres.

Find the right word(s) in the text above for each of the clues below:

1. Bordeaux in France is famous for these alcoholic drinks

2. An alcoholic drink which is made from apples

3. An adjective, other than fizzy, used to describe water with bubbles of gas in it

4. A piece of paper, attached to a product, with information on it

5. A type of beer that's a darker colour than lager

6. Sugar is made from a tropical plant called sugar cane and so is this spirit

7. An adjective that describes drinks that don't have any alcohol in them

8. Scotland is famous for this alcoholic drink

9. This spirit originally came from Russia

10. Water that isn't sold in bottles (2 words)

11. An word used to describe drinks which are supposed to make us feel less tired

12. An adjective used for any drinks which have bubbles of gas in them

13. A drink which is made by adding water to a small amount of concentrated fruit juice

14. Just over half a litre of beer in a large glass

15. An adjective used for drinks made from the leaves and flowers of plants

/ 15

136. Breakfast and Brunch

In the UK we usually have breakfast quite soon after we get up. As we get up at different times, breakfast can be any time from about 6am to 10am. Some people have cereal or porridge. If they're hungry, they might also have bread or toast with butter and marmalade, or jam. Others have a cooked breakfast, which may include a selection of bacon, vegetarian, vegan or pork sausages, eggs, tomatoes, mushrooms and baked beans. The eggs are usually fried, scrambled or poached, but boiled eggs can be eaten on their own or with a piece of toast and butter. Hot drinks such as tea and coffee are drunk at breakfast, and cold drinks, like orange juice, are too.

There's a meal between breakfast and lunch which is called brunch. The word 'brunch' is a combination of the first two letters of 'breakfast' and the last four letters of 'lunch'. Not everyone eats brunch. Some people have brunch when they get up too late for breakfast, so it's perfect if you've had a late night. The food can be similar to breakfast, or very different, often more like lunch. Ham, cheese, boiled eggs, yogurt / yoghurt / yoghourt, fruit and bread are frequently served as brunch, and this type of food is available in most hotels either for breakfast or brunch.

Find the right word(s) in the text above for each of the clues below:

1. Breakfast and brunch are two examples of this

2. Eggs which are mixed with a little milk and cooked in a saucepan

3. Eggs which are cooked in their shells in very hot water

4. Eggs which are cooked without their shells in very hot water

5. Eggs which are cooked with a little oil in a frying pan

6. Bacon and sausages come from a pig and so does this other meat

7. Apples, oranges and pears are all types of this food

8. We buy these in tins. They're normally in a tomato sauce (2 words)

9. Cornflakes and muesli are both types of this food

10. Two or more things that are mixed or put together

11. This is a type of jam made of oranges or other fruit, which is popular in the UK

12. Bread that's been heated and turned brown

13. This white food is cooked with water or milk and eaten hot with a little sugar or honey on top

14. We spread this on bread, toast and hot sweetcorn

15. This word has a similar meaning to 'often'

/ 15

137. Lunch, Tea, and Supper

Most of us have breakfast in the morning, lunch in the middle of the day, and supper, or dinner, in the evening. When we go out to a restaurant in the evening, the meal is normally called dinner, especially on more formal occasions. Supper is an informal evening meal at home, so most of us have supper much more often than dinner.

For formal lunch and dinner there may be three courses: a starter, a main course and a dessert. There's often a choice, too, between a dessert and cheese. At work, though, most people have less time for a meal. It's possible to carry on working after only a short break if you have a sandwich or a snack which is quick and easy to eat. This is very different from lunch in a restaurant, or Sunday lunch at home, which takes a lot longer.

Tea is a light meal which people have in the afternoon, at about 4 or 5pm. It might just be a cup of tea with a piece of cake or a couple of biscuits, but sometimes there are sandwiches instead. In the UK, the names people use for meals can be confusing. Different words are used for meals in the north of England, and early supper, especially for children, is called tea in many family homes across the country.

Find the right word(s) in the text above for each of the clues below:

1. The first course of a meal in a restaurant

2. Meat or fish with vegetables or a salad which is served in the middle of a meal (2 words)

3. Apple pie and custard, strawberries and cream, and sticky toffee pudding are all examples of this course

4. A small amount of food which is eaten between meals

5. Two slices of bread with cheese, ham, tomatoes, egg or some other filling in the middle

6. An adjective which describes a relaxed meal at home with friends or family

7. An adjective which describes a meal, clothes, or words, which are suitable or right for a particular occasion

8. If you're having these with a cup of tea, take a few of them out of the packet and put them on a small plate

9. If you're having this with a cup of tea, cut it into slices and give a piece of it to anyone who'd like one

10. An adjective which describes a small meal. It's the opposite of 'heavy'

11. Difficult to understand

12. Later than the morning, but earlier than the evening

13. A period of time when we stop what we're doing to rest, or eat something

14. A dairy product that comes from cows and goats

15. Continue (2 words)

/ 15

138. Cooking at Home

This is my recipe for spaghetti Bolognese. Start by taking a large onion. Peel, slice, and then chop it into small pieces. I always wear swimming goggles when I do this, so the onions don't sting my eyes and make me cry. Heat a couple of tablespoons of olive oil in a large saucepan, add the onions and fry them gently. While this is happening, take some garlic, remove the skin, and put it through a garlic crusher. When the onions have gone brown, add some minced beef, which we call mince, and fry it for about a minute next to the onions. Pour half a litre of water into the saucepan, mix it with the mince and the onions until it boils, and leave it all to simmer on a low heat. Put the garlic and some tinned tomatoes in the saucepan. Add a beef stock cube, a glass of red wine and three or four bay leaves to the mixture. Stir the contents of the saucepan carefully with a wooden spoon every ten minutes and cook the sauce on a low heat for at least an hour.

Now take a chunk of Parmesan cheese and grate it into a small bowl. Cut some parsley into small pieces with a pair of scissors and put it in another bowl. Boil a kettle and pour the water into a separate saucepan. Take the spaghetti from the packet and cook it in the boiling water for about ten minutes. When the spaghetti is soft, separate it from the water with a sieve. Now serve the spaghetti and the sauce with the cheese and parsley on top.

Find the right word(s) in the text above for each of the clues below:

1. This breaks garlic into tiny pieces (2 words)

2. What you do with a spoon to mix food in a mug, a bowl or a saucepan

3. I use parsley and this other herb in my recipe (2 words)

4. The opposite of 'hard'

5. Water does this at 100 degrees Celsius

6. Cook food in a saucepan, but on a low heat so it doesn't boil

7. These are bigger than dessert spoons and much bigger than teaspoons!

8. Everything in a container

9. Break carrots or cheese into tiny pieces using a metal object

10. This could be beef, chicken, lamb or vegetable and is added to sauces and soups (2 words)

11. Remove the skin from a fruit or a vegetable

12. Cut food like bread, ham or onions into thin pieces

13. Cut food with a quick downwards action

14. Cook quickly in a pan, using oil or butter

15. This tells you how to cook a dish or some food

/ 15

139. Eating in Restaurants

When you go into a restaurant, there's normally a waiter to greet you. If it's a popular restaurant it's always best to book a table in advance. The waiter might ask you whether you've booked and then take you to your table, or try to find you one. Once you've sat down, you'll be able to look at the menu and order some drinks. In some restaurants there are tablecloths and napkins on the tables and there's normally cutlery for every customer. There may also be salt, pepper and slices of bread. Read the menu carefully and decide how many courses you would like. If you're hungry you could have a starter, a main course and a dessert, or cheese at the end of the meal. The waiter serves all your food and drink at your table, unless there's a buffet, in which case you help yourself, or it's a fast-food restaurant, where you take what you've chosen to your table.

Once you've finished eating and are ready to leave, ask the waiter for the bill. When it's brought to your table you'll need to tell the waiter how you want to pay. If you're paying by debit or credit card the waiter will use a card machine so you can make your payment. Service is usually included, but if it's not, you may wish to give the waiter a tip for serving you.

Find the right word(s) in the text above for each of the clues below:

1. Another way of saying 'reserve' a table

2. Starters and desserts are examples of these

3. Forks, knives and spoons

4. If you haven't eaten for seven or eight hours this is how you might feel

5. Assistance that customers get from people who work in restaurants, shops and hotels

6. Read this before you choose what you'd like to eat

7. A piece of paper that tells you how much you have to pay for your meal

8. This is given to waiters by some customers for good service

9. A formal verb used to welcome someone or say 'hello' to them

10. The opposite of 'arrive'

11. Pieces of paper or cloth used to wipe your mouth or fingers when you're eating

12. Tell the waiter what you would like to eat and drink

13. Before something happens or you do something (2 words)

14. An adjective used to say a lot of people like or enjoy something

15. A powder that's a spice and is usually grey or black. We put it on food so it tastes better

/ 15

140. Food from Other Countries

In London and other capital cities you can try food from a lot of different countries in the world. The UK is famous for its fish and chips, and it's also known for roast beef and Yorkshire pudding. But it's the food from other countries that gives people so much choice. Couscous is a North African food, from countries like Algeria and Morocco, which is normally eaten with meat or vegetables. Moules frites, French for mussels and chips, is a Belgian dish which is also common in France. Crepes, or pancakes, are popular in France too, and even snails and frogs' legs are eaten there! The Germans have brought us their sausages, their frankfurters were named after the city of Frankfurt, and hamburgers were named after Hamburg. Pastries, which can be bought in most bakers' and coffee shops, are called Danish pastries because they were originally from Denmark.

Greek restaurants serve specialities like moussaka, Indian ones offer a selection of curry dishes with rice, and the Italians are famous all over the world for their pizza and pasta. If you go to a Spanish restaurant you can eat some of their tapas dishes, and if you like raw fish you'll enjoy Japanese sushi. There are too many foods from around the world to list them all here. But if you spend time in a city like London or Paris, why not try as many of them as you can?

Find the right word(s) in the text above for each of the clues below:

1. A dish that's made with aubergine, minced meat and cheese (on the top)

2. The word 'moules' in English

3. This adjective means 'uncooked'

4. Spaghetti and ravioli are two types of this food

5. The English word for a food that's made of flour, eggs and milk and cooked in a frying pan

6. This is also made from flour, eggs and milk but it's baked in an oven (2 words)

7. Raw fish served with rice or vegetables

8. Use money to pay for something, or time to do something

9. Patatas bravas, chorizo and tortilla are three types of this food, which is served on small plates

10. Shops that sell bread and pastries

11. Toulouse, salami and merguez

12. Sweet cakes which are made of pastry and have fruit or nuts on top or in the middle (2 words)

13. This food is cooked with cheese on top of bread, and small pieces of meat and vegetables on top of the cheese

14. A meat or vegetable dish from South East Asia which is usually cooked with spices

15. Small, soft animals that move very slowly and have hard, round shells

/ 15

SHOPPING AND SHOPS

141. The History of Shopping

Shopping has been a human activity for thousands of years. In ancient Greece and Rome there were places called markets where people could buy things. There were stalls in the markets where everything on sale was displayed so customers could examine the goods and decide what they wanted. Even then, people had a good idea of what they were going to buy before they arrived at the market. We know this because the earliest known shopping list in the UK was written about two thousand years ago by a Roman soldier. It was discovered near Hadrian's Wall, which is in Northumberland, a county in the north of England.

The first shops with windows which displayed goods were in London in the late 18th century. Shop owners realised they needed to attract customers so they used advertisements and arranged everything they wanted to sell in their shop windows. In the 19th century the first department stores were opened with a wide range of items in different departments. Later on, shopping centres were built indoors so customers could walk from one shop to another in the same building. Some shopping centres are in cities or towns, but others can be found outside urban areas.

Find the right word(s) in the text above for each of the clues below:

1. Showed people goods by putting them in places where they could easily be seen

2. People who buy things from shops, stores or companies

3. An adjective used for, or to do with, a town or a city

4. All the things you need to buy, when you go shopping, written on a piece of paper (2 words)

5. Very old, or from a period of time thousands of years in the past

6. Large shops divided into departments with different types of goods in each one (2 words)

7. Tables with things arranged on them to be sold at a market

8. Products which are bought and sold

9. Inside a building

10. Look at something very closely and carefully to see what it's like

11. Information about products, with pictures, intended to attract and interest people

12. Available to be bought (2 words)

13. Places outside or inside buildings where goods are bought and sold

14. Make people so interested in something that they want to have it

15. The activity of going to a shop or a store and buying things

/ 15

142. Shops

Department stores and supermarkets in the UK sell a large number of different goods, and almost anything can be bought online. Many of the shops in shopping centres and the high street, however, specialise in one type of product. There are clothes shops, sports shops and toy shops, bakers' that sell bread, and coffee shops that can make you a coffee. Jewellers' display jewellery like rings and watches, and florists' sell flowers. Pet shops have plenty of things for dogs, cats and rabbits. If you're looking for something for your home or garden, go to your furniture shop, hardware store, or gardening centre, and for something old and interesting, try the antique shop. Stationery shops are useful for work, school and free time, and electrical shops can help you with all those appliances in the flat.

In recent decades, computer stores, phone shops and fast food places have appeared on our streets. Fast food restaurants sell hamburgers, chicken, or sandwiches, and some offer healthy food too. Why not buy your meat at the local butcher's, though, or your vegetables at the greengrocer's? You can get your medicines or anything you want to keep in your bathroom from your local chemist's, and the estate agents on the high street will help you find a property. If you need just one or two everyday items, the convenience store on the corner of your street is the place to go.

There used to be a shop for almost everything, but not anymore. Online shopping and companies that deliver anything you need to your home are changing the way shopping is done. Shops are closing down every day, especially in our high streets, because they can't make any money.

Find the right word(s) in the text above for each of the clues below:

1. This shop sells fruit and vegetables

2. Large buildings with a number of different shops inside (2 words)

3. If you want to buy an old painting you might find one here (2 words)

4. These shops sell pens, rulers and paper (2 words)

5. Go and see these people if you need somewhere to live (2 words)

6. TVs and washing machines, light bulbs and plugs, are on sale in these places (2 words)

7. The main road in a town (2 words)

8. A shop that sell tables, chairs and sofas (2 words)

9. Chicken, beef, pork and lamb are sold in this shop

10. Medicines, shampoo and toothpaste can be bought here

11. If you need a lawnmower, a wheelbarrow or a potted plant, go to this place (2 words)

12. This shop is very near home. It sells newspapers, sandwiches, cold drinks and tinned food (2 words)

13. A word used for things that are bought and sold

14. Equipment and tools for DIY (do it yourself) jobs at home are sold here (2 words)

15. This means the same as 'kind' or 'sort'

/ 15

143. Clothes Shopping

When I went into the clothes shop, all the shop assistants were busy helping other customers. This gave me time to look at the clothes that were on sale and see if there was anything that I liked enough to buy. There was a shirt and a pair of trousers that I liked, but they were the wrong size. A shop assistant finished serving another customer and walked over to me. She smiled and asked me whether she could help. I showed her the clothes I had found and explained that I needed a different size. She said she would check whether they had my size in stock in the storeroom. As soon as she had gone, another assistant offered to help me. I thanked her, but said that I was already being served. The first assistant then came back carrying a shirt on a hanger. She said the trousers were out of stock but she had found a shirt that was my size. I told her I'd like to try it on, so she took me to the changing rooms.

The shirt fitted me perfectly. I looked in the mirror to check whether it suited me as well. I thought it looked good on me so I decided to buy it, took it off, and put my own one back on. When I came out of the changing room I told the assistant that I would take the shirt I'd just tried on. We went over to the cash desk where she took the shirt and put it in a plastic bag. She asked me if I would like to order some trousers in my size, so I did. Then I paid for my new shirt, thanked her for her help, and left the shop.

Find the right word(s) in the text above for each of the clues below:

1. Words that go before socks, shoes, gloves, trousers and shorts (2 words)

2. All the products that aren't displayed in the shop are kept here

3. A piece of flat glass that we see ourselves in if we stand in front of it

4. This person's job is to help you find what you need when you go shopping (2 words)

5. Being helped by someone working in a shop, a bank or a restaurant (2 words)

6. This means it 'was the right size for me' (2 words)

7. This means it 'looked good on me' (2 words)

8. Something that's either too large, or too small (2 words)

9. Things we've bought can be carried in this (2 words)

10. This means something is either 'in the shop or the storeroom' (2 words)

11. This means something isn't in the shop or the storeroom (3 words)

12. Put a shirt on this and hang it in a wardrobe

13. A verb that's often used instead of 'buy' to say we're going to buy something in the shop

14. You need to do this if you want a shop assistant to get you something which is out of stock

15. This is where we go to pay in a shop (2 words)

/ 15

144. Supermarkets

Before you go to the supermarket, it's a good idea to check what you need and write a shopping list. If there isn't a supermarket near where you live, you'll need to go to one by car or public transport. Large supermarkets normally have car parks which customers can use, and unlike other car parks, are free. When you arrive at the entrance of the supermarket, get a trolley if you're going to do a lot of shopping, or a basket if you only need a few things. You can attach your shopping list to the front of some trolleys, which makes shopping easier. If you know where everything is, you'll find what you're looking for quickly. Fruit and vegetables are usually in the same area, and meat and fish are nearby. Dairy products like milk and yogurt / yoghurt / yoghourt are all together, and so are most tinned soups, meat, fish and vegetables. Pasta, cereals, biscuits and tea are mostly in packets and much of this food is likely to be on shelves in one or two of the aisles. Drinks are all in the same location as well, with bottles and cans of soft drinks near alcoholic ones, like beer, wine and spirits.

You can buy almost anything in a supermarket. If there's something you need for your family, dog or cat, your kitchen or your bathroom, you'll find it there. There's always a lot of fresh food, but plenty of frozen food as well. If you choose anything from a supermarket freezer, though, make sure you put it in your trolley just before you go to the check out to pay. If you do, it should still be frozen when you get home!

Find the right word(s) in the text above for each of the clues below:

1. A plastic or metal container that you carry round a supermarket and put your shopping in

2. A large metal container with four wheels that you push round a supermarket and put your shopping in

3. An adjective used for food in small metal containers

4. Paper or cardboard containers for food

5. This service has buses and trains that take you where you need to go (2 words)

6. This word means that you don't have to pay for something

7. Food which is zero degrees Celsius!

8. This is where you go into a place. it's the opposite of the 'exit'

9. A piece of paper with all the things you need to buy written on it (2 words)

10. Spaghetti and ravioli are two types of this food

11. Cornflakes, muesli and granola

12. Whisky, gin and vodka

13. These are like corridors but they're in supermarkets and churches, and on planes

14. The place where you pay for your shopping in a supermarket (2 words)

15. People who buy things in a shop or a supermarket

/ 15

145. Shopping Online

Shopping online gives us more information about different products than we've ever had before. If you're looking for something online, use a search engine to find the companies that sell it. Price comparison sites compare how much different companies are charging for the same product. Do some research on these sites and you're likely to pay less than if you just walked into a shop and bought the product. Online shopping's convenient too. You can shop anywhere and at any time, day or night.

Although it helps if someone you know recommends a product, it's important to read the reviews written by customers about a company, before you decide whether to buy or pay for something. By doing this, you often learn a lot more about the quality of a product or a service, and the number of stars given by customers can also be helpful. I recently found a company that had excellent reviews and provided me with a very good product and service. Their website had all the information I needed and I was able to search for and find exactly what I wanted. I entered my personal details online, made the payment and purchased the product. They sent several texts to inform me where the product was and when it would be delivered. It arrived at my home address in less than 24 hours.

Customers, though, can have a very different experience when they shop online. If you read about a company and the reviews warn you about awful service or terrible products, that's probably what you'll get. Don't waste any time or money on companies with bad reviews. They may get back to you quickly if you want to buy a product, but some of them are very difficult, if not impossible to reach if you try to contact them about a problem with a product you've already bought. If you're still unsure about a company after reading their reviews, why not send them an email or a text, or call them, to see how they respond?

Find the right word(s) in the text above for each of the clues below:

1. A noun used to say how good (or bad) something is

2. Examine two or more things to find out how similar or different they are

3. Google and Yahoo are examples of this (2 words)

4. Look for something (2 words)

5. Look at these online if you want to find the cheapest option (3 words)

6. Names, addresses and phone numbers (2 words)

7. Useful, easy and quick to do or use

8. Tells someone how good, useful or enjoyable something is and suggests they try it

9. Another word for 'bought'

10. Sent or taken to a place

11. Put information into a computer

12. People's written opinions of products or services they didn't like (2 words)

13. Do this to find out and learn as much as you can about something

14. Not certain

15. In reviews these are usually between one and five

/ 15

PEOPLE

146. What Women Wear

In the morning when we get up, we get dressed, or put on our clothes. During the day we wear our clothes. Before we go to bed at night, we get undressed, or take off our clothes.

Women wear underwear, which is normally a bra and knickers. Over their underwear, some women wear jeans, trousers or shorts, with a shirt or T-shirt. Others wear dresses, or a blouse and a skirt. Businesswomen and women at work tend to wear formal clothes, such as a suit, which is a jacket with matching trousers or a matching skirt. Women also wear stockings or tights, but when it's cold, or to go running or play sports, many prefer leggings. In winter, like men, they may also wear a sweater, and put on a coat, a hat and a scarf when they go out. On their feet they wear shoes or boots, with gloves on their hands to keep them warm.

More women than men wear jewellery. They wear necklaces and earrings, rings on their fingers, and bracelets on their wrists. Women also wear make-up, and we use the same verbs to describe how it's worn as the verbs that are used for wearing clothes. Women put make-up on in the morning, wear it during the day or in the evening and then take it off. There are many different types of make-up, but two of the most popular are lipstick and mascara.

Find the right word(s) in the text above for each of the clues below:

1. Metal or plastic objects that people wear as decoration

2. Clothing that women or girls wear that hangs from the waist

3. A casual, cotton shirt with short sleeves

4. This has a collar, long sleeves and buttons, and is worn over a shirt or a blouse

5. Having clothes, jewellery or make-up on

6. Clothing women wear on their legs, which is made of thicker material than stockings and tights

7. Trousers which are made of denim

8. Make-up that women wear around their mouths

9. These clothes, worn by women rather than men, cover most of the body above and below the waist

10. An adjective used for clothes worn at work, or on official or special occasions

11. A type of shirt worn by women rather than men

12. A piece of cloth we wear around our necks in cold weather

13. The same colour and made of the same material

14. Strong shoes that cover the lower part of the leg and the foot

15. Worn over other clothes to keep us dry or warm when we go out

/ 15

147. What Men Wear

In the morning, when we get up, we get dressed, or put on our clothes. During the day we wear our clothes. Before we go to bed at night, we get undressed, or take off our clothes.

The general word for underwear that most men wear is pants, (the long word is underpants), and there's a choice of boxer shorts, trunks, or briefs. When it's cold, some men wear a vest. Over these clothes they usually wear a shirt above the waist, and trousers below it, but when it's hot, or when they're playing sports, a lot of men wear shorts. Businessmen used to wear a formal shirt and a tie, but nowadays most men who are at work prefer to undo the top button of their shirt instead. Many of them wear a jacket over the shirt, or a suit, which is a jacket and matching trousers. When men are at home they wear more casual clothes, and a lot of young men wear jeans, a T-shirt and trainers. Men usually wear socks and shoes on their feet. Most shoes are black or brown, but they can be any colour. Some shoes have laces and others don't.

Find the right word(s) in the text above for each of the clues below:

1. A small round piece of plastic or metal which we can do up or undo

2. Pants and vests

3. This is a cotton shirt with short sleeves, and most of them don't have any buttons

4. The same colour and made of the same material

5. The opposite of formal

6. Put on our clothes (2 words)

7. Shoes that people wear to play sports or for informal occasions

8. Wore something in the past, but not any longer (3 words)

9. These need to be done up, (on some pairs of shoes), and undone before they're taken off

10. Underwear which some people wear under a shirt

11. A long, narrow piece of cloth which some men wear at the front of a shirt

12. A noun used for a type of underwear, or what men wear when they go swimming

13. A belt is worn around this part of the body

14. These are worn over our feet and inside our shoes

15. Clothes, worn by both men and women, that cover the body from the waist to the ankle of each leg

/ 15

148. The Body

For students learning English, it's useful to learn the words used for different parts of the body. One way of doing this is to describe which parts are next to each other. Every human body has a head, (at the top), which contains a brain, which we use to think. At the top of the head we have hair, (except bald men and some babies). Our ears are on each side of the head, and at the front there's a face with two eyes, a nose and a mouth. Below the mouth is a chin, and below the chin is a neck, which connects the head to the rest of the body. The front of the neck is called the throat.

Below the neck is a chest, (at the front), and a back, (at the back). Human beings have shoulders on each side which are at the top of our arms. We bend our arms at the elbows, and at the end of our arms there are hands. On each hand we have four fingers and a thumb. Below the chest is the stomach, which is above the waist. Below the waist on each side are our hips, which are just above the bottom, (which is below the back). Below the bottom we have two legs, which bend at our knees. At the end of the legs are two feet, and in between each leg and each foot there's a part of the body called the ankle. Each foot has five toes. This ends our journey from head to toe!

Find the right word(s) in the text above for each of the clues below:

1. These are between the upper and lower parts of the arm

2. Similar to a finger, but shorter and thicker

3. This controls how we move, feel, think and remember

4. Food and air go through this on their way from the head to the body

5. One of the five small parts of the body at the front of the foot

6. This adjective is about people rather than animals or machines

7. A belt is worn around this part of the body

8. Move an arm or a leg so it's no longer straight

9. An adjective used to describe a person who has no hair, (or very little hair) on their head

10. This is where the top and bottom half of legs are joined

11. A part of the body between the head and the shoulders

12. This is just above the foot and below the leg

13. The front part of the body, below the neck and above the stomach

14. These are at the top of the arms

15. A part of the body that a man can grow a beard on

/ 15

149. The Family

The day my sister got married, the weather couldn't have been better. The sun was shining, and the skies above were bright blue. The wedding ceremony was in a beautiful, old church in the village.

At the end of the service, we walked slowly out of the church. The photographer approached us, and asked us all to pose for photos with the bride and groom. I've still got some of the photos, and they remind me how special the occasion was. There's one in particular I like. Almost everyone in the family is in the picture. My sister and her new husband are in the front row, in the middle. My mother and father are standing beside them, and my mother's parents, (my grandmother and grandfather), are also at the front, next to my father. My aunt, uncle, older brother, and my nephew and niece, are all in the background, in the row behind. My cousin, who's the same age as I am, is standing just in front of my uncle. All the members of the groom's family are on the other side of the newly-wed couple. I know who they are now, but I didn't on the day of the wedding. I'd met my new brother-in-law on several occasions, but the first time I met other members of his family was at the reception.

Find the right word(s) in the text above for each of the clues below:

1. My father's or mother's sister

2. My father's or mother's brother

3. Help me to remember (2 words)

4. This person's job is to take photos

5. A formal religious occasion when two people are married (2 words)

6. The woman who gets married, on the day of the wedding

7. Family and friends usually go to this after the wedding to celebrate

8. At the back of a picture or a photo

9. A number of people standing or sitting next to each other, or chairs positioned next to each other

10. My uncle's or aunt's child

11. My sister's husband

12. The man who gets married, on the day of the wedding

13. My brother's or sister's daughter

14. My brother's or sister's son

15. Sit or stand to be photographed, painted or drawn

/ 15

150. Life and Death

There's a saying that only two things are certain in life: death and taxes. It was said by Benjamin Franklin in the 18th century, and it could be true today. We still pay taxes, and we're not here forever. Let's make the most of every day, be kind to other people, and work hard at everything we do.

There's also a prayer that says we should accept the things we can't change, and have the wisdom to change the things we can. Death is the normal and natural end of life. There's nothing we can do about it. We can, however, change the lives of elderly people, and the experience of those at the end of their lives. In recent decades there have been global reports on the quality of life for people over the age of sixty. The reports have concluded that the elderly in countries like Switzerland, Norway and Sweden, have better health, pensions, employment and care than anywhere else. The rest of the world can learn from these countries. Governments have a responsibility to make sure people in need receive proper care, especially when they become ill or frail in old age.

People who are suffering or in pain can now be given better medical treatment and drugs than at any time in history, so their experience is less painful and difficult. With advances in medical science, a priority this century should be to make dying as painless as possible for those who are near the end of life. And when someone dies, we should remember they are at peace, before, during, and after the funeral. Finally, if it's their wish, let's throw their ashes into the wind, in a place they once loved.

Find the right word(s) in the text above for each of the clues below:

1. An obligation to do something

2. An adjective with the same meaning as 'old', which is used to describe people

3. The ability to make good decisions because of the knowledge and experience we have

4. No longer worried or troubled (by mental or physical pain) (2 words)

5. An adjective used to say nothing hurts, either mentally or physically

6. Physically weak and in poor health

7. Money we pay to the government so it can pay for public services

8. With a lot of effort

9. Caring about others and being friendly and generous

10. A religious ceremony for someone who has died

11. Suggest we should do something

12. The powder that remains after something has been burnt

13. A noun used for the words people say to their God, often to give thanks or ask for help

14. The end of life

15. Continue with a difficult situation, or something we don't like, because it can't be changed

/ 15

ANSWERS

···

Adults *(Topic 59)*
1. decades
2. hairstyle
3. pastimes
4. public transport
5. save
6. spend
7. furniture
8. recycle
9. plays
10. adopt
11. wear
12. social media
13. grown up
14. throw things away
15. pets

Airports *(Topic 87)*
1. departure
2. arrival
3. screens
4. hand luggage
5. hold
6. board
7. allowed
8. plane
9. passport
10. on time
11. delayed
12. gate
13. terminal
14. customs
15. airline

Alexander Fleming *(Topic 5)*
1. discovered
2. visible
3. dish
4. mushroom
5. by mistake
6. pile
7. infection
8. lids
9. laboratory
10. antibiotics
11. researcher
12. treat
13. basement
14. sealed
15. sorting through

American Politics *(Topic 24)*
1. policies
2. guns
3. member
4. taxes
5. military spending
6. laws
7. senators
8. population
9. senior
10. health care
11. death penalty
12. right-wing
13. left-wing
14. constitution
15. republic

An Evening In *(Topic 80)*
1. higher
2. curtains
3. home delivery
4. central heating
5. documentaries
6. curry
7. weather forecast
8. sweater
9. bills
10. news
11. comedy
12. dark
13. take away
14. cosy
15. radiators

Bank Accounts *(Topic 127)*
1. prove
2. building societies
3. accounts
4. interest rate
5. current account
6. savings account
7. in debit
8. in credit
9. branch
10. percentage
11. overdraft allowance
12. interest
13. spend
14. insurance
15. benefits

Barbara Jordan *(Topic 19)*
1. keynote
2. authority
3. achieve
4. belief
5. lawyer
6. obstacles
7. suffer
8. obligation
9. impeachment
10. privileges
11. in her own right
12. remove
13. innovation
14. gap
15. reject

Bathroom Things *(Topic 74)*
1. antiseptic cream
2. washbag
3. toothbrush
4. plasters
5. run out of
6. bathroom cabinet
7. flannel
8. deodorant
9. mirror
10. shaving foam
11. razor
12. shower gel
13. aftershave
14. scissors
15. soap

Biology *(Topic 46)*
1. DNA
2. roots
3. breathing
4. genus
5. respiration
6. habitats
7. ecosystems
8. nutrition
9. cells
10. reproduction
11. genes
12. digestion
13. circulation
14. hormones
15. nerves

Birds *(Topic 108)*
1. blood
2. nightingales
3. parrots
4. extinction
5. ostriches
6. penguins
7. flocks
8. beak
9. creatures
10. feathers
11. migrate
12. teeth
13. visual
14. pink
15. species

Boats *(Topic 88)*
1. yachts
2. oceans
3. voyages
4. cruise ships
5. the Channel
6. cabins
7. lifeboats
8. rowing boats
9. goods
10. portholes
11. canals
12. seafood
13. lakes
14. cargo ships
15. ports

Breakfast and Brunch *(Topic 136)*
1. meal
2. scrambled
3. boiled
4. poached
5. fried
6. ham
7. fruit
8. baked beans
9. cereal
10. combination
11. marmalade
12. toast
13. porridge
14. butter
15. frequently

British Politics *(Topic 21)*
1. general election
2. education
3. elected
4. transport
5. majority
6. half
7. head
8. the Cabinet
9. democracy
10. prime minister
11. constituency
12. state
13. represents
14. votes
15. combined

Care for the Elderly *(Topic 29)*
1. frailty
2. carers
3. stairlifts
4. old
5. disability
6. get dressed
7. lonely
8. dependence
9. activities
10. installed
11. dementia
12. care homes
13. well
14. enable
15. charities

Cats and Dogs *(Topic 107)*

1. sociable
2. fur
3. fetch
4. carried
5. string
6. claws
7. paws
8. ignores
9. hunted
10. drop
11. exercise
12. picked up
13. commands
14. packs
15. patting

Charles Dickens *(Topic 13)*

1. corrupt
2. working conditions
3. factory
4. rejection
5. debt
6. overcrowded
7. poverty
8. no doubt
9. backgrounds
10. social status
11. improve
12. strange
13. suited
14. novels
15. prison

Chemistry *(Topic 47)*

1. carbon
2. organic
3. liquids
4. gases
5. electricity
6. tiny
7. universe
8. petrochemical
9. polymer
10. pharmaceutical
11. dots
12. inorganic
13. reactions
14. invented
15. discovered

Children *(Topic 57)*

1. sit
2. raise
3. alphabet
4. dance
5. birthday
6. cry
7. triangles
8. teenagers
9. fingers
10. crawl
11. vocabulary
12. stand
13. laugh
14. draw
15. development

Cities *(Topic 81)*

1. nightlife
2. underground railways
3. department stores
4. museums
5. outskirts
6. capital cities
7. commuters
8. skyscrapers
9. rush hour
10. airports
11. parks
12. art galleries
13. crowded
14. theatres
15. suburbs

Climate Change *(Topic 119)*

1. droughts
2. breathe
3. rock
4. factories
5. coal
6. icebergs
7. deserts
8. forests
9. fossil fuels
10. temperature
11. erupt
12. oil
13. heatwaves
14. melting
15. storms

Clothes Shopping *(Topic 143)*

1. pair of
2. storeroom
3. mirror
4. shop assistant
5. being served
6. fitted me
7. suited me
8. wrong size
9. plastic bag
10. in stock
11. out of stock
12. hanger
13. take
14. order
15. cash desk

Coaches and Trains *(Topic 94)*

1. sharing
2. destination
3. helicopter
4. afford
5. disadvantage
6. north
7. west
8. coach station
9. carriages
10. exhausting
11. option
12. petrol
13. buffet
14. within
15. journeys

Colds and Flu *(Topic 31)*

1. influenza
2. sore
3. rises
4. symptoms
5. stay
6. carry on
7. viruses
8. headache
9. infectious
10. temperature
11. spreads
12. throat
13. sneeze
14. chest
15. fever

Communication *(Topic 55)*

1. gesture
2. non-verbal
3. wink
4. blink
5. raise
6. clap
7. thumb
8. glance
9. stare
10. abroad
11. point
12. eyebrows
13. blush
14. wave
15. expressions

Computing *(Topic 50)*

1. camera
2. computer programs
3. mouse
4. case
5. sounds
6. memory
7. drive
8. scanner
9. keyboard
10. monitor
11. tablets
12. codes
13. instructions
14. processes
15. speakers

Continents and Countries *(Topic 111)*

1. quarter
2. fifth
3. three quarters
4. permanently
5. size
6. the largest
7. the least populated
8. vast
9. areas
10. ice
11. Africa
12. covered
13. Canada
14. Brazil
15. China

Cooking at Home *(Topic 138)*

1. garlic crusher
2. stir
3. bay leaves
4. soft
5. boils
6. simmer
7. tablespoons
8. contents
9. grate
10. stock cube
11. peel
12. slice
13. chop
14. fry
15. recipe

Crime *(Topic 36)*

1. arsonists
2. terrorists
3. terrible
4. drug dealer
5. hidden
6. burglars
7. robbers
8. rapist
9. murderer
10. stolen
11. muggers
12. hijackers
13. victim
14. valuables
15. serious

Democracies and Elections *(Topic 25)*

1. constituency
2. dictator
3. opinion polls
4. protests
5. demonstrations
6. polling
7. candidates
8. speeches
9. alternative
10. force
11. publicity
12. broadcasts
13. adverts
14. vote
15. policies

Disability *(Topic 28)*
1. wheelchairs
2. ago
3. sports events
4. psychological
5. physical
6. available
7. caring
8. injured
9. function
10. limbs
11. prevent
12. impairment
13. inherited
14. challenge
15. artificial

Disasters *(Topic 118)*
1. disasters
2. famine
3. drought
4. property
5. emergency aid
6. collapse
7. drown
8. floods
9. buildings
10. cut off
11. road accident
12. earthquake
13. suddenly
14. spread
15. destroyed

Diseases in Poor Countries *(Topic 32)*
1. wrong
2. health education
3. lose their lives
4. dirty
5. poverty
6. health care
7. tuberculosis
8. sick

9. quickly
10. malaria
11. infect
12. immune systems
13. crowded
14. diseases
15. tragic

Diseases in Rich Countries *(Topic 33)*
1. forms
2. fatal
3. desk
4. cancer
5. overweight
6. heart disease
7. diet
8. cured
9. exercise
10. strokes
11. fat
12. sugar
13. heart attacks
14. diagnosed
15. blood vessel

Doctors and Chemists *(Topic 34)*
1. counter
2. tablets
3. worried
4. surgery
5. strong
6. prescription
7. diagnose
8. ache
9. treatment
10. appointment
11. referred
12. register
13. specialist
14. knowledge
15. examine

Drinks *(Topic 135)*
1. wines
2. cider
3. sparkling
4. label
5. bitter
6. rum
7. soft
8. whisky
9. vodka
10. tap water
11. energy
12. fizzy
13. squash
14. pint
15. herbal

Earning Money *(Topic 128)*
1. goes up
2. increase
3. afford
4. transport
5. rent
6. cash
7. tax
8. following
9. minimum
10. hard
11. transferred
12. promotion
13. employment contract
14. tax return
15. desks

Earth and Other Planets *(Topic 115)*
1. closest to
2. exist
3. Mars
4. Venus
5. rock
6. boil
7. freeze
8. Saturn
9. orbit
10. distance
11. rings
12. space
13. provides
14. conditions
15. gas

Eating in Restaurants *(Topic 139)*
1. book
2. courses
3. cutlery
4. hungry
5. service
6. menu
7. bill
8. tip
9. greet
10. leave
11. napkins
12. order
13. in advance
14. popular
15. pepper

Education *(Topic 60)*
1. history
2. exams
3. English
4. universities
5. maths
6. degree
7. chemistry
8. primary school
9. option
10. design and technology
11. assessment
12. geography
13. biology
14. nursery school
15. physics

Education, Health, and Benefits *(Topic 30)*
1. maternity benefit
2. unemployment benefit
3. adoption payment
4. pension
5. rent
6. income support
7. state schools
8. short
9. retirement
10. reached
11. treatment
12. health care
13. expensive
14 welfare state
15. disabled

Emergencies *(Topic 37)*
1. charged
2. violent
3. flashing
4. disobey
5. handcuffs
6. emergency
7. dialling
8. paramedic
9. bail
10. accident
11. offence
12. arrested
13. witnesses
14. sirens
15. in custody

Emmeline Pankhurst *(Topic 16)*
1. militant
2. meetings
3. campaigns
4. repeatedly
5. prison
6. battle
7. suffragettes
8. speech
9. hunger strikes
10. inequality
11. elections
12. vote
13. property
14. hardest
15. audience

Employment *(Topic 62)*
1. pension
2. shortlisted
3. education
4. salary
5. annual leave
6. personal details
7. employees
8. retire
9. position
10. recruitment
11. qualifications
12. employer
13. assess
14. experience
15. training

English Grammar *(Topic 41)*
1. prepositions
2. adverbs
3. function
4. rules
5. conjunctions
6. suitable
7. verbs
8. nouns
9. sentences
10. types
11. pronouns
12. parts of speech
13. adjectives
14. register
15. determiners

English Vocabulary *(Topic 42)*

1. make sure
2. teachers
3. understand
4. meaning
5. at home
6. properly
7. question
8. dictionary
9. exercises
10. online
11. pronounce
12. many
13. right
14. explaining
15. books

Entertainment *(Topic 67)*

1. romantic
2. current affairs
3. soap operas
4. documentaries
5. comedies
6. horror films
7. action films
8. switch on
9. thrillers
10. series
11. available
12. quiz shows
13. technology
14. drama
15. channels

Extreme Weather *(Topic 124)*

1. extremely
2. forecasts
3. equator
4. torrential
5. prevent
6. hurricanes
7. thousand
8. shocked
9. blizzards
10. tropical air
11. floods
12. droughts
13. thunderstorms
14. heatwaves
15. destruction

Finding Accommodation *(Topic 76)*

1. estate agent
2. higher up
3. landlords
4. mortgage
5. ground floor flat
6. accommodation
7. property
8. basement flat
9. lodger
10. let
11. afford
12. lift
13. block of flats
14. signs
15. tenants

Finding Work *(Topic 61)*

1. hard
2. initial
3. challenges
4. experience
5. temporary
6. candidates
7. promotion
8. employer
9. qualifications
10. education
11. successful
12. opportunity
13. competitive
14. stressful
15. realistic

Fish and Seafood *(Topic 132)*

1. wrapped
2. tins
3. sole
4. prepare
5. catch
6. versatile
7. sardines
8. crab
9. flour
10. mussels
11. delicious
12. salmon
13. haddock
14. popular
15. oysters

Food from other Countries *(Topic 140)*

1. moussaka
2. mussels
3. raw
4. pasta
5. pancakes
6. Yorkshire pudding
7. sushi
8. spend
9. tapas
10. bakers'
11. sausages
12. Danish pastries
13. pizza
14. curry
15. snails

Fruit *(Topic 134)*

1. strawberries
2. bananas
3. pineapple
4. grapes
5. peaches
6. melon
7. cherries
8. pips
9. apples
10. raspberries
11. kiwifruit
12. prepare
13. squeeze
14. bowl
15. greengrocer's

Furniture *(Topic 78)*

1. sofa bed
2. antique shop
3. sofa
4. armchair
5. chest of drawers
6. bookcase
7. desk
8. cupboard
9. grandfather clock
10. stool
11. wardrobe
12. dressing table
13. lamp
14. modern
15. painting

Gambling *(Topic 130)*

1. chance
2. live
3. crime
4. available
5. addiction
6. roulette
7. cards
8. bet
9. steal
10. lottery
11. casino
12. risk
13. anxiety
14. depression
15. desperate

Gardens *(Topic 79)*
1. greenhouse
2. weeds
3. lawn
4. neighbours
5. gardening gloves
6. stored
7. wheelbarrow
8. spade
9. fork
10. soil
11. shed
12. patio
13. fences
14. hosepipe
15. hedges

Gears and Pedals *(Topic 92)*
1. engine
2. fourth
3. park
4. press
5. reverse
6. faster
7. accelerator
8. clutch
9. brake
10. handbrake
11. wheels
12. pedal
13. reduce
14. slope
15. operate

Geoffrey Chaucer *(Topic 11)*
1. scissors
2. entertainment
3. astronomer
4. literature
5. prose
6. verse
7. theatre
8. desk
9. messenger
10. abroad
11. pilgrims
12. philosopher
13. characters
14. documents
15. poets

George Orwell *(Topic 14)*
1. regime
2. pen name
3. opposed
4. express
5. opinions
6. control
7. dictator
8. totalitarian
9. journalist
10. force
11. turns against
12. rules
13. civil war
14. popular
15. influenced by

Giving Directions *(Topic 83)*
1. take
2. pub
3. shop
4. keep
5. sign
6. bends
7. forks
8. bridge
9. directions
10. turn
11. footpath
12. past
13. get to
14. map
15. pointing

Growing Up *(Topic 58)*
1. used to
2. shape
3. free time
4. decisions
5. feelings
6. parents
7. teenagers
8. lasts
9. vocabulary
10. attracted to
11. views
12. rely
13. identity
14. argue
15. worry

Having a Baby *(Topic 56)*
1. ante-natal
2. the safest
3. equipment
4. health centre
5. suffer
6. looking after
7. birth
8. pregnant
9. sickness
10. midwives
11. makes them
12. vomit
13. resources
14. maternity ward
15. is born

Henry VIII *(Topic 8)*
1. jealous
2. religion
3. seeing
4. executed
5. ruled
6. divorce
7. painting
8. marriage

9. the pope
10. punished
11. allowed
12. preferred
13. showed
14. arranged
15. lucky

Hobbies *(Topic 69)*
1. leisure
2. jewellery
3. at home
4. camping
5. metal detecting
6. cooking
7. chess
8. models
9. indoors
10. pastimes
11. gardening
12. kites
13. coins
14. Monopoly
15. stamps

Holidays *(Topic 89)*
1. slopes
2. seaside
3. helmets
4. campsites
5. water-skiing
6. sailing
7. the Alps
8. goggles
9. sunbathe
10. ski resort
11. sticks
12. boots
13. diving
14. snow
15. surfing

Hospitals *(Topic 35)*
1. overnight
2. wards
3. intensive care
4. paramedic
5. maternity
6. relative
7. treatment
8. accident
9. stands for
10. set off
11. casualty
12. burns
13. cuts
14. cancer
15. medical insurance

Houses *(Topic 77)*
1. office
2. urban
3. flight of stairs
4. detached
5. dining room
6. bungalows
7. terraced
8. attic
9. elderly
10. utility room
11. rural
12. semi-detached
13. reach
14. hall
15. corridor

How Animals Look *(Topic 102)*
1. look
2. fur
3. reptiles
4. amphibians
5. patterns
6. purple
7. grey
8. ginger
9. beard
10. prehistoric
11. lizards
12. pink
13. behave
14. rainbow
15. bright

How Animals Move *(Topic 103)*
1. gallop
2. swim
3. slither
4. hop
5. forwards
6. climbing
7. squirrels
8. ground
9. kangaroos
10. crawl
11. wasps
12. evolved
13. flying
14. quickly
15. swing

How Animals Sound *(Topic 104)*
1. buzz
2. chirping
3. purr
4. whine
5. trumpet
6. bark
7. chatter
8. cluck
9. crow
10. growl
11. baa
12. squeak
13. croak
14. neigh
15. quack

Howard Carter *(Topic 4)*

1. priceless
2. pharaohs
3. chisel
4. archaeologist
5. sealed
6. search
7. intact
8. dig
9. discovered
10. tomb
11. steps
12. candle
13. guarding
14. ebony
15. statues

How We Look *(Topic 52)*

1. fit
2. stubble
3. beard
4. moustache
5. slim
6. wavy
7. curly
8. identical
9. overweight
10. parting
11. ginger
12. hairstyles
13. tall
14. diet
15. plaits

How We Move *(Topic 53)*

1. lean
2. tremble
3. jump
4. climb
5. shiver
6. turn
7. swim
8. crawl
9. stroll
10. wander
11. shrug
12. limp
13. march
14. fall
15. run

How We Sound *(Topic 54)*

1. terrified
2. hilarious
3. exhausted
4. furious
5. cough
6. sneeze
7. snore
8. burp
9. scream
10. puff and pant
11. giggle
12. hum
13. whistle
14. groan
15. sigh

How We Think *(Topic 51)*

1. humour
2. reptiles
3. personality
4. mammals
5. reasoning
6. brains
7. instincts
8. early
9. adapted
10. abstract thought
11. relied
12. pleasure
13. memories
14. responsibility
15. creative

Insects *(Topic 109)*
1. land
2. bite
3. itchy
4. butterflies
5. wasps
6. drink
7. prevent
8. annoying
9. pesticides
10. locusts
11. honey
12. sleeves
13. horsefly
14. sting
15. damage

Interviews *(Topic 63)*
1. apply
2. motivation
3. appointment
4. confident
5. unemployed
6. shoes
7. positive
8. convince
9. appearance
10. interview
11. clean
12. expressions
13. application
14. enthusiastic
15. professional

Isaac Newton *(Topic 2)*
1. telescope
2. plague
3. rainbow
4. pulled
5. published
6. force
7. motion
8. the Moon
9. rates
10. mirrors
11. realised
12. gravity
13. composed
14. laws
15. wondered

JK Rowling *(Topic 15)*
1. published
2. cope
3. character
4. magical
5. wizards
6. pen name
7. orphan
8. in parallel with
9. crowded
10. evil
11. story
12. skills
13. delayed
14. series
15. copies

Jobs *(Topic 65)*
1. interior designer
2. chef
3. dentist
4. architect
5. farmer
6. journalist
7. engineer
8. estate agent
9. accountant
10. career
11. IT
12. temporary
13. au pairs
14. receptionist
15. skills

Kitchen Things *(Topic 75)*
1. larder
2. dishcloth
3. bowls
4. hob
5. go off
6. dairy products
7. boiled
8. cutlery
9. crockery
10. baking tray
11. ready meals
12. stored
13. mugs
14. tea towel
15. kitchen utensils

Languages *(Topic 113)*
1. Brazil
2. widely
3. billion
4. population
5. Hispanic
6. considered to be
7. large
8. India
9. Canada
10. Hindi
11. Portuguese
12. Spanish
13. Arabic
13. Mandarin
15. business

Learning to Drive *(Topic 91)*
1. passenger's seat
2. allowed
3. indicator
4. signal
5. by hand
6. qualified
7. licence
8. reverse
9. safely
10. instructor
11. practise
12. pass
13. roundabout
14. mirrors
15. turn

Leonardo da Vinci *(Topic 1)*
1. tourists
2. calculator
3. genius
4. helicopter
5. inventor
6. satellites
7. parachute
8. contact lenses
9. machine gun
10. invisible
11. bridge
12. hurricanes
13. discovered
14. robots
15. tanks

Life and Death *(Topic 150)*
1. responsibility
2. elderly
3. wisdom
4. at peace
5. painless
6. frail
7. taxes
8. hard
9. kind
10. funeral
11. let's
12. ashes
13. prayer
14. death
15. accept

Local Government *(Topic 27)*

1. leisure
2. waste
3. the environment
4. running
5. elderly
6. disabled
7. the emergency services
8. at risk
9. income tax
10. council tax
11. value
12. services
13. properties
14. extension
15. related to

Looking after Children *(Topic 98)*

1. kettles
2. knock them over
3. pavement
4. pan handles
5. fireworks
6. cupboards
7. swallowing
8. close
9. sharp
10. suffocation
11. barbecue
12. dangerous
13. drawers
14. temperature
15. toddlers

Lunch, Tea, and Supper *(Topic 137)*

1. starter
2. main course
3. dessert
4. snack
5. sandwich
6. informal
7. formal
8. biscuits
9. cake
10. light
11. confusing
12. afternoon
13. break
14. cheese
15. carry on

Martin Luther King *(Topic 18)*

1. campaign
2. nation
3. segregation
4. march
5. poverty
6. civil rights
7. led
8. inspired
9. assassinated
10. rooted in
11. brotherhood
12. minister
13. resistance
14. slaves
15. in his honour

Maths *(Topic 49)*

1. rates
2. equals
3. lines
4. multiplication
5. division
6. addition
7. subtraction
8. percentages
9. angles
10. quantities
11. symbols
12. measurements
13. calculations
14. population
15. surfaces

Matilda *(Topic 6)*
1. claim
2. prevented
3. civil war
4. army
5. monasteries
6. lowered
7. captured
8. escape
9. heavily
10. safety
11. death
12. coronation
13. throne
14. attacked
15. Holy Roman Emperor

Meat *(Topic 131)*
1. beef
2. lamb
3. pork
4. suffer
5. duck
6. steak
7. tastes
8. processed
9. minced
10. roast
11. stews
12. sausage
13. bacon
14. lasagne
15. chops

Medical Emergencies *(Topic 96)*
1. bleeding
2. ambulance
3. bruise
4. the police
5. paramedics
6. stroke
7. at once
8. recovery

9. unconscious
10. burn
11. sting
12. bite
13. first aid kits
14. lips
15. poisonous

Michael Faraday *(Topic 3)*
1. vacuum cleaners
2. fossil fuels
3. chlorine
4. mechanical
5. poor
6. renewable
7. pull
8. reverse the process
9. fridges
10. discovery
11. nuclear
12. motor
13. experiments
14. benzene
15. achievement

Money and Currencies *(Topic 126)*
1. shape
2. exchange rates
3. worth
4. notes
5. coins
6. pounds sterling
7. yen
8. currencies
9. recognise
10. research
11. euro
12. peso
13. check
14. count
15. compare

Music *(Topic 68)*

1. violin
2. studio
3. wealthy
4. piano
5. vocalists
6. drums
7. choir
8. solo artists
9. talented
10. saxophone
11. downloaded
12. orchestra
13. recording contract
14. voices
15. guitar

Numbers and Calculations *(Topic 44)*

1. decade
2. centilitres
3. times
4. 52
5. equals
6. combination
7. common
8. calculators
9. 75
10. 23
11. century
12. cards
13. symbol
14. tend
15. easier

Oceans *(Topic 112)*

1. the Southern Ocean
2. dolphins
3. surface
4. size
5. seafood
6. area
7. whales
8. sharks
9. deep
10. salt
11. depend on
12. weighs
13. put together
14. creatures
15. the Indian Ocean

Pedestrians and Cyclists *(Topic 100)*

1. motorists
2. cyclists
3. pedestrians
4. motorcyclists
5. dark
6. traffic
7. traffic lights
8. traffic island
9. helmets
10. the safest
11. accidents
12. pedestrian crossings
13. overtake
14. lorries
15. visibility

People at Work *(Topic 64)*

1. full time
2. information technology
3. human resources
4. customer services
5. public relations
6. sales
7. marketing
8. self-employed
9. managing director
10. colleagues
11. part time
12. permanent
13. accountant
14. majority
15. companies

Physics *(Topic 48)*
1. geothermal
2. forces
3. squashed
4. accelerates
5. universe
6. solar
7. potential
8. electromagnetic
9. fossil fuels
10. nuclear
11. speed
12. shape
13. microwave ovens
14. renewable
15. batteries

Places to Visit in London *(Topic 85)*
1. the Tower of London
2. deer
3. the London Eye
4. fun
5. the National Gallery
6. the Science Museum
7. London Zoo
8. paintings
9. Kew Gardens
10. St Paul's Cathedral
11. the Elizabeth Tower
12. Buckingham Palace
13. cruise
14. Richmond Park
15. tour

Planes and Flying *(Topic 86)*
1. crew
2. stationary
3. accelerates
4. heavy
5. safety demonstration
6. taking off
7. landing
8. engines
9. powerful
10. get off
11. luggage
12. flight
13. wings
14. undo
15. towards

Plants *(Topic 110)*
1. roots
2. branches
3. seasons
4. cardboard
5. oxygen
6. aspirin
7. useful
8. cotton
9. shampoo
10. stem
11. fences
12. trunk
13. carbon dioxide
14. boats
15. rubber

Poverty and Hunger *(Topic 117)*
1. starve
2. housing
3. desert
4. desperate
5. rain
6. health care
7. possessions
8. agriculture
9. poverty
10. disease
11. thirsty
12. hungry
13. survive
14. disasters
15. aid

Preventing Burglaries *(Topic 99)*

1. garages
2. neighbourhood
3. burglar alarm
4. have trouble
5. valuable
6. strong
7. properties
8. locks
9. burglars
10. deter
11. thick
12. climbing
13. fence
14. visible
15. prevent

Public Transport *(Topic 93)*

1. the busiest
2. traffic jams
3. boat
4. escalators
5. deck
6. hire
7. bikes
8. above
9. lifts
10. destination
11. in a hurry
12. stations
13. underground railway
14. convenient
15. lines

Punishment and Prison *(Topic 40)*

1. court
2. suspended sentence
3. fine
4. death sentence
5. theft
6. judge
7. attend
8. sentences
9. guilty
10. behind bars
11. serious
12. reoffend
13. charged
14. behave
15. unpaid

Richard III *(Topic 7)*

1. skeleton
2. DNA
3. army
4. protect
5. throne
6. marriage
7. illegal
8. famous
9. murder
10. play
11. arranged
12. buried
13. ordered
14. battle
15. agree

Safaris, Zoos, and Farms *(Topic 106)*

1. welfare
2. organic
3. habitat
4. extinct
5. cruel
6. poaching
7. dairy products
8. wool
9. elephants
10. escape
11. survive
12. buffaloes / buffalo
13. hunt
14. goats
15. wild

Safety at Home *(Topic 97)*

1. flexes
2. plugs
3. cookers
4. appliances
5. candles
6. ladders
7. clutter
8. trip
9. slip
10. lawnmowers
11. conducts
12. dustpan
13. bare
14. smoke alarm
15. spread

Safety on the Roads *(Topic 95)*

1. traffic lights
2. pedestrian crossings
3. motorists
4. motorcyclists
5. cyclists
6. pedestrians
7. helmet
8. thinking of
9. flashing
10. improve
11. scene
12. protect
13. tragic
14. ambulance
15. siren

Samuel Pepys *(Topic 9)*

1. disaster
2. infected
3. administering
4. fleas
5. destroyed
6. damaged
7. the Tower of London
8. rats
9. diary
10. servant
11. witnessed
12. view
13. fire
14. spread
15. experiences

Shapes and Sizes *(Topic 45)*

1. circles
2. slices
3. collar
4. huge
5. triangles
6. squares
7. rectangles
8. roundabouts
9. shape
10. measurements
11. waist
12. the right size
13. wheels
14. mention
15. tiny

Shopping Online *(Topic 145)*

1. quality
2. compare
3. search engine
4. search for
5. price comparison sites
6. personal details
7. convenient
8. recommends
9. purchased
10. delivered
11. entered
12. bad reviews
13. research
14. unsure
15. stars

Shops *(Topic 142)*
1. greengrocer's
2. shopping centres
3. antique shop
4. stationery shops
5. estate agents
6. electrical shops
7. high street
8. furniture shop
9. butcher's
10. chemist's
11. gardening centre
12. convenience store
13. goods
14. hardware store
15. type

Sightseeing and Tourism *(Topic 90)*
1. sightseeing
2. play
3. free of charge
4. cathedrals
5. get lost
6. art gallery
7. fountains
8. souvenirs
9. tourist office
10. tourist
11. castles
12. markets
13. brochures
14. statues
15. show

Spending Money *(Topic 129)*
1. budget
2. in credit
3. debit card
4. interest
5. expensive
6. compare
7. overdrawn
8. loan
9. avoid
10. spent
11. owe
12. in debt
13. bill
14. overdraft allowance
15. finished

Sports and Places *(Topic 70)*
1. court
2. water polo
3. front
4. motor racing
5. athletics track
6. pitches
7. grass
8. empty
9. diving boards
10. stadium
11. rugby
12. professionals
13. racecourse
14. venues
15. higher

Sports Equipment *(Topic 71)*
1. swimsuit
2. shuttlecock
3. cue
4. equipment
5. expensive
6. table tennis
7. snooker
8. helmet
9. boots
10. clubs
11. table
12. goggles
13. oval
14. pair of
15. bicycle

Stephen Hawking *(Topic 20)*

1. paralysed
2. interview
3. role model
4. physicist
5. run of the mill
6. motor neurone disease
7. perceptions
8. cosmologist
9. transforming
10. creativity
11. career
12. charter
13. fundraising
14. diagnosed
15. encouragement

Supermarkets *(Topic 144)*

1. basket
2. trolley
3. tinned
4. packets
5. public transport
6. free
7. frozen
8. entrance
9. shopping list
10. pasta
11. cereals
12. spirits
13. aisles
14. check out
15. customers

The Animal Family *(Topic 101)*

1. camels
2. whales
3. giraffes
4. deer
5. crocodiles
6. feed
7. cows
8. tortoises
9. squirrels
10. give birth
11. rabbits
12. seal
13. dolphins
14. whiskers
15. amazed

The Arts *(Topic 66)*

1. ballet
2. museums
3. novels
4. paintings
5. classical
6. biographies
7. poems
8. audience
9. drawings
10. short stories
11. sculptures
12. ceramics
13. refers to
14. plays
15. opera

The Body *(Topic 148)*

1. elbows
2. thumb
3. brain
4. throat
5. toe
6. human
7. waist
8. bend
9. bald
10. knees
11. neck
12. ankle
13. chest
14. shoulders
15. chin

The Countryside *(Topic 82)*

1. valleys
2. ponds
3. farms
4. hills
5. wild
6. cottages
7. quieter
8. crops
9. villages
10. scenery
11. streams
12. fields
13. woods
14. flat
15. fresh air

The Courts *(Topic 39)*

1. crime
2. witnesses
3. permitted
4. arguing
5. murder
6. rape
7. robbery
8. in custody
9. convicted
10. acquitted
11. Crown Court
12. evidence
13. defends
14. prosecutes
15. examination

The Environment *(Topic 120)*

1. the environment
2. rubbish
3. protect
4. attic
5. electrical appliances
6. plastic bags
7. brush
8. central heating
9. electricity
10. cans
11. recycle
12. wastes
13. nearby
14. charity shop
15. transported

The European Union *(Topic 23)*

1. referendum
2. currency
3. price
4. agriculture
5. services
6. improve
7. fisheries
8. immigration
9. borders
10. laws
11. goods
12. inflation
13. energy supply
14. crime
15. trade

The Family *(Topic 149)*

1. aunt
2. uncle
3. remind me
4. photographer
5. wedding ceremony
6. bride
7. reception
8. background
9. row
10. cousin
11. brother-in-law
12. groom
13. niece
14. nephew
15. pose

The Forecast (Topic 125)
1. Wales
2. Scotland
3. milder
4. rise
5. scattered
6. patches
7. high
8. isolated
9. widespread
10. outlook
11. dry
12. coasts
13. frost
14. sleet
15. ice

The Four Seasons (Topic 123)
1. hours
2. showers
3. May
4. June
5. October
6. February
7. drier
8. mild
9. sunrise
10. sunset
11. the coldest
12. unsettled
13. snows
14. sunshine
15. storms

The History of Shopping (Topic 141)
1. displayed
2. customers
3. urban
4. shopping list
5. ancient
6. department stores
7. stalls
8. goods
9. indoors
10. examine
11. advertisements
12. on sale
13. markets
14. attract
15. shopping

The Industrial Revolution (Topic 10)
1. steam
2. engines
3. invented
4. textiles
5. the poorest
6. communications
7. techniques
8. railway lines
9. iron
10. steel
11. factories
12. canals
13. coal
14. trading
15. education

The Police (Topic 38)
1. witnesses
2. evidence
3. recorded
4. report
5. on foot
6. victims
7. on duty
8. shifts
9. demonstrations
10. investigations
11. uniform
12. detective
13. community
14. statements
15. search

The Seaside *(Topic 84)*

1. shallow
2. seagulls
3. crabs
4. horizon
5. view
6. nets
7. island
8. towels
9. lifeguards
10. sunglasses
11. yachts
12. sunbathe
13. bay
14. coast
15. suncream

The Welfare State *(Topic 26)*

1. employment
2. earn
3. income
4. benefits
5. wealth
6. advised
7. pensions
8. education
9. health care
10. fairer
11. poverty
12. reformer
13. unemployed
14. housing
15. opportunities

Tools *(Topic 72)*

1. hammer
2. carpenters
3. plug
4. remove
5. repair
6. screwdriver
7. drill
8. surface
9. screws
10. hole
11. nail
12. toolbox
13. tightened
14. pastime
15. electrical appliance

UK Political Parties *(Topic 22)*

1. left-wing
2. right-wing
3. policies
4. taxes
5. majority
6. debt
7. public services
8. cuts
9. the House of Commons
10. transport
11. public spending
12. priority
13. coalition
14. poorer
15. billions

Vegetables *(Topic 133)*

1. spinach
2. beans
3. mushrooms
4. broccoli
5. peppers
6. vitamins
7. salads
8. salad dressing
9. carrots
10. lettuce
11. combination
12. cucumber
13. sprouts
14. cauliflower
15. peas

Wars *(Topic 116)*
1. throughout
2. innocent
3. fight
4. victims
5. on foot
6. weapon
7. peace
8. destroy
9. sunk
10. invaded
11. civilians
12. wounded
13. bombs
14. battles
15. submarines

What Men Wear *(Topic 147)*
1. button
2. underwear
3. T-shirt
4. matching
5. casual
6. get dressed
7. trainers
8. used to wear
9. laces
10. vest
11. tie
12. trunks
13. waist
14. socks
15. trousers

What Weather! *(Topic 122)*
1. predict
2. storms
3. windy
4. icy
5. cloudy
6. thunder
7. lightning
8. snow
9. skies
10. soaked
11. warm
12. cosy
13. forecast
14. freezing
15. complain

What Women Wear *(Topic 146)*
1. jewellery
2. skirt
3. T-shirt
4. jacket
5. wearing
6. leggings
7. jeans
8. lipstick
9. dresses
10. formal
11. blouse
12. scarf
13. matching
14. boots
15. coat

William Shakespeare *(Topic 12)*
1. mistakes
2. mistaken identity
3. civil war
4. cause
5. actors
6. syllables
7. theatres
8. misunderstanding
9. comedies
10. sad
11. stage
12. centuries
13. ruled
14. argue
15. rhyme

Winston Churchill *(Topic 17)*

1. enemy
2. dangerous
3. coalition
4. surrender
5. broadcasts
6. confidence
7. appointment
8. toil
9. sweat
10. tears
11. gratitude
12. turning the tide
13. speeches
14. survival
15. defend

Words for Feelings *(Topic 43)*
(Someone or something is....)
1. interesting
2. amusing
3. disappointing
4. annoying
5. terrifying
(I'm /I feel....)
6. ashamed
7. delighted
8. tired
9. frightened
10. embarrassed
11. bored
12. pessimistic
13. optimistic
14. happy
15. proud

Words for Weather *(Topic 121)*

1. baking
2. refreshing
3. chilly
4. hurricanes
5. winds
6. freezing

7. breeze
8. mild
9. boiling
10. higher
11. stopped
12. downpour
13. warm
14. damp
15. gales

Work and School *(Topic 73)*

1. scissors
2. eraser
3. paper clips
4. laptop
5. stapler
6. whiteboard
7. correction pen
8. files
9. sharpener
10. highlighters
11. stationery
12. ruler
13. notebook
14. printer
15. bin

World Records *(Topic 105)*

1. the oldest
2. the heaviest
3. the slowest
4. oceans
5. speed
6. peregrine falcon
7. whales
8. giraffes
9. cheetahs
10. tortoises
11. ostriches
12. share
13. centuries
14. native to
15. explorer

World Religions *(Topic 114)*

1. believers
2. prophet
3. Catholics
4. agnostics
5. Islam
6. Christianity
7. Hinduism
8. Buddhists
9. ago
10. atheists
11. Protestants
12. calm
13. silence
14. exists
15. normally

INDEX OF TOPICS

Printed in Great Britain
by Amazon